Subsidia et Instrumenta Linguarum Orientis

(SILO)

Herausgegeben von / Edited by
Reinhard G. Lehmann / Robert M. Kerr

2

2014
Harrassowitz Verlag · Wiesbaden

Annick Payne

Hieroglyphic Luwian

An Introduction with Original Texts

3rd Revised Edition

2014

Harrassowitz Verlag · Wiesbaden

For further information about the glyphs on the cover consult page 217.

Bibliografische Information der Deutschen Nationalbibliothek
Die Deutsche Nationalbibliothek verzeichnet diese Publikation in der Deutschen
Nationalbibliografie; detaillierte bibliografische Daten sind im Internet
über http://dnb.dnb.de abrufbar.

Bibliographic information published by the Deutsche Nationalbibliothek
The Deutsche Nationalbibliothek lists this publication in the Deutsche
Nationalbibliografie; detailed bibliographic data are available in the internet
at http://dnb.dnb.de.

For further information about our publishing program consult our
website http://www.harrassowitz-verlag.de

Printed on permanent/durable paper.
Logo: Semitic inscription on the top of a foundation nail. Period of the Amorite
Kingdoms (2004–1595 BCE). Larsa, Babylon. © akg-images/Erich Lessing.
Printing and binding: docupoint, Barleben
Printed in Germany
ISSN 1867-8165
ISBN 978-3-447-10216-2

Contents

Preface

This book aims to offer an affordable yet comprehensive introduction to Hieroglyphic Luwian. Because this subject is not widely taught the book has been designed to equip a beginner with the necessary knowledge to pursue autodidactic study. Based on the current state of research, this book aims to give a – necessarily selective - overview of the text corpus, to familiarise the reader with the reference tools and secondary literature, to introduce some common problems and to build up a basic understanding of the signs, grammar and vocabulary. Texts are therefore not presented with a highly critical commentary, and some more problematic passages have been purposefully omitted, although enough difficulties will be encountered to alert the reader to some of the problems involved. Excluded is the study of Bronze Age Inscriptions, seal legends and accompanying iconography. Since references to secondary literature also needed to be selective, only the most important, comprehensive and up-to-date treatments have been included.

Apart from the reference sections (Abbreviations, Vocabulary, Sign List and Bibliography) the book divides into three parts, namely Introduction, Grammar and Texts. The first part introduces the language, inscriptions, research history and available reference tools. The second part provides a short overview of the grammar. The third part consists of twelve sample texts, both shorter inscriptions and excerpts from longer ones. Each text is presented with an introduction, translation with grammatical analysis and a review section. The sample texts have been chosen to illustrate the most common literary topics of the hieroglyphic text corpus, and to introduce the basic vocabulary and the most frequent signs in a variety of shapes. Grammatical explanations and vocabulary notes build up with every text. The following symbols are used for simplification: ☞ (note), 📖 (further reading), ❧ (review). The Vocabulary section provides a basic glossary of Hieroglyphic Luwian including all words encountered in the texts of this book. The Sign List contains all signs with their current values.

Writing this book would not have been possible without the help and advice of the following: First and foremost, I wish to thank Prof. Dr. G. Neumann, whose kindness in reading the manuscript with his customary sharp eye, giving detailed comment, and generously and patiently discussing many issues has contributed greatly. A great debt of gratitude goes to Prof. J. D. Hawkins, who provided valuable input and insights and without whose teaching I could never have undertaken this work. I am grateful to Dr. L. d'Alfonso for his many acute observations and his encouragement, to Prof. Dr. H. Nowicki for discussion of various points, and to the students with whom I have used the work in draft form. I would also like to thank Dr. J. Marzahn, Prof. Dr. J. Renger and Dr. B.

Salje for the opportunity to study objects at the Vorderasiatisches Museum, Berlin. Many thanks to my husband for his invaluable computer support and unfailing sympathy and consideration during all stages of the book. The revised second edition incorporates recent research and has greatly benefited from the most generous input of Prof. Craig Melchert on problems big and small. I would also like to thank Dr. Ilya Yakubovich for his feedback. I am indebted to Dr. R. G. Lehmann, editor of the 'Subsidia et Instrumenta Linguarum Orientis' series and to the team at Harrassowitz. While much error has been eliminated, I am keenly aware that imperfections remain and they are my responsibility alone.

Annick Payne
September 2009

The third edition includes some corrections and references to recent developments in Luwian studies. I have updated the contents in accordance with the latest findings, with the exception of the new readings proposed by Rieken–Yakubovich 2010, which I do not wish to adopt at this stage; nonetheless, references are included where applicable. Likewise, I do not adopt the suggestion of Simon 2008 regarding the reading of the sign *448.

I would like to thank the following for comments and for sharing their work with me: Lorenzo d'Alfonso, Federico Giusfredi, Craig Melchert, Alice Mouton, Zsolt Simon, Ilya Yakubovich.

Annick Payne
June 2013

Abbreviations

1. Bibliographical

AfO	*Archiv für Orientforschung.*
Anatolica	*Anatolica*, Annuaire international pour les civilisations de l'Asie anterieure, publie sous les auspices de l'institut historique et archeologique néerlandais a Istanbul, Leiden.
AnSt	*Anatolian Studies.* Journal of the British Institute of Archaeology at Ankara.
BSL	*Bulletin du Musée de Beyrouth.*
CAH	*The Cambridge Ancient History.*
CHLI	Hawkins, J.D., *Corpus of Hieroglyphic Luwian Inscriptions*, Volume I, Inscriptions of the Iron Age, Berlin/New York, 2000.
DBH	*Dresdner Beiträge zur Hethitologie*, Dresden.
Fs	*Festschrift.*
Fs Krahe	*Sybaris*, Festschrift Hans Krahe, Wiesbaden 1958.
Fs Güterbock	Hoffner, H.A. and Beckman, G.M. (ed.), 1986, *Kaniššuwar, A tribute to Hans G. Güterbock on his seventy-fifth Birthday, May 27, 1983*, Assyriological Studies 23, Chicago.
Fs Neumann	Tischler, J. (ed.), 1982, *Serta Indogermanica. Festschrift für Günter Neumann zum 60. Geburtstag*, Innsbruck.
Fs Otten	Neu, E and Rüster, C. (ed.), 1973, Festschrift Heinrich Otten, Wiesbaden.
Fs Szemerényi	Broganyi, B. (ed.), 1979, *Studies in Diachronic, Synchronic and Typological Linguistics. Festschrift für Oswald Szemerényi on the Occasion of his 65th Birthday*, Amsterdam.
Gs	*Gedenkschrift.*
Gs Carter	Arbeitman, Y.L. (ed.), The Asia Minor Connexion: Studies on the Pre-Greek Languages in Memory of Charles Carter, *Orbis* Supplementa 13, Leuven-Paris, 2000.
Gs Herter	Erbse, H. (et al. ed.), TIMHTIKOS TOMOS Hans Herter, Athens 1988.
Gs Kronasser	Neu, E. (ed.), 1982, *Investigationes Philologicae et Comparativae. Gedenkschrift für Heinz Kronasser*, Wiesbaden.
HdO	*Handbuch der Orientalistik.* Boston/Leiden.
HS	s. *KZ*
IncLing	*Incontri Linguistici*, Università degli studi di Trieste, Firenze.
JIES	*Journal of Indo-European Studies.*

JRAS	*Journal of the Royal Asiatic Society of Great Britain and Ireland.*
Kadmos	*Kadmos.* Zeitschrift für vor- und frühgriechische Epigraphik.
Kratylos	*Kratylos.* Kritisches Berichts- und Rezensionsorgan für indogermanische und allgemeine Sprachwissenschaft.
KZ	*(Kuhns) Zeitschrift für vergleichende Sprachforschung* 1-100 (1952-1987), renamed *Historische Sprachforschung,* abbr. *HS* (1988 -).
MAOG	*Mitteilungen der Altorientalischen Gesellschaft.*
MSS	*Münchner Studien zur Sprachwissenschaft.*
MVAG	*Mitteilungen der vorderasiatisc Gesellschaft.* Leipzig.
MVAeG	*Mitteilungen der vorderasiatisch-ägyptischen Gesellschaft.* Leipzig.
Or	*Orientalia.* Rome.
Oriens	*Oriens.* Journal of the International Society for Oriental Research.
RHA	*Revue hittite et asianique.*
SAOC	*Studies in Ancient Oriental Civilizations.* Chicago.
SMEA	*Studi micenei ed egeo-anatolico.* Rome.
Sprache	*Die Sprache.* Zeitschrift für Sprachwissenschaft.
StBoT	*Studien zu den Boğazköy-Texten.* Wiesbaden.
Studies Cowgill	Watkins, C. (ed.), 1987, *Studies in Memory of Warren Cowgill. Papers from the Fourth East Coast Indo-European Conference, Cornell University, June 6-9, 1985*, Berlin/New York.
Syria	*Syria*, Revue d'art oriental et d'archéologie, publiée par l'Institut français d'archeologie du Proche-Orient, Beyrouth.
WAW	*Writings from the Ancient World*, Society of Biblical Literature. Atlanta.
WZKM	*Wiener Zeitschrift für die Kunde des Morgenlandes.*

2. General

*	(prefixed to a numeral) sign number after Laroche 1960b
*	(prefixed to a word) reconstructed word or form
X	unclear logogram
x	unclear syllabogram
§	clause
|	word-divider
||	line end
-'	word end
ͥ	personal determinative
" "	logogram marker

⌐ ¬	signs partially preserved
[ ]	signs not preserved
< >	scribal error: signs omitted
<< >>	scribal error: omit signs
⧬	review
⌗	reference for further reading
☞	note

a.	accusative
abl.	ablative
act.	active
AD	anno domini
adj.	adjective
adv.	adverb
BC	before Christ
c.	circa
C	common gender
caus.	causative
conj.	conjunction
cpt	connective particle
CL	Cuneiform Luwian
comm.	comment
compl.	complement
conj.	conjunction
d.	dative
dem.	demonstrative
det.	determinative
dir.obj.	direct object
disj.	disjunctive
DN	divine name
ed.	edited/editor
e.g.	exempli gratia
encl.	enclitic
esp.	especially
eth.	ethnic suffix
g.	genitive
GN	geographical name
hgl.	hieroglyphic
Hitt.	Hittite
HL	Hieroglyphic Luwian
IE	Indo-European
i.e.	id est

ind.	indicative
ind.obj.	indirect object
indef.	indefinite
inf.	infinitive
intr.	intransitive
imp.	imperative
iter.	iterative
log.	logogram
lpt.	locative particle
Luw.	Luwian
med.-pass.	medio-passive
mut.	mutation-*i*
N	neuter
n.	Nominative
n.e.	no ending
neg.	negative
npt	neuter particle
num.	numeral
p.adj.	possessive adjective
part.	participle
pers.	personal
ph.i.	phonetic indicator
phon.	phonetic
pl.	plural
PN	personal name
poss.	possessive
postpos.	postposition
prev.	preverb
pron.	pronoun
prs.	present
prt.	preterite
pt.	particle
qpt.	quotative particle
rel.	relative
RN	royal name
s.	see
s.u.	see under
sg.	singular
subj.	subject
suff.	suffix
trs.	transitive
v.	verb

1   Introduction

1.1   Language and Inscriptions

1.1.1   Luwian

The term 'Hieroglyphic Luwian' refers to a language and a writing system, namely Luwian written in a hieroglyphic script. The Luwian language is one of several Luwic languages, a group belonging to the Anatolian branch of the Indo-European language family and related to Hittite, Palaic and Lydian. The Luwic languages comprise Lycian A and Lycian B (also called 'Milyan'), Carian, Pisidian and Sidetic as well as Luwian. Of the latter, several dialects were recorded in two scripts, Ancient Near Eastern cuneiform and a hieroglyphic script used solely – with the exception of foreign personal names – for Luwian. Recent research shows that linguistically, there is evidence for at least three Luwian dialects, namely Kizzuwatnian, Empire and Iron Age Luwian. The latter a direct descendant from Empire Luwian, the dialect favoured by the administration at Hattusa. As all surviving texts are the product of either bureaucratic institutions or high standing individuals such as merchants, they must by nature represent the language of an elite rather than a common vernacular.

Scholars agree that the Indo-European speakers represent a group intrusive to Anatolia but opinions differ greatly as to where the original homeland of these peoples lay, when and by what route they arrived in Anatolia and when they separated into individual language groups. As they continued to live in close proximity, one should not view this separation as isolating but rather expect continued reciprocal linguistic influences and exchange.

☞ *Terminology*: Older publications sometimes refer to 'Hittite Hieroglyphic'which is not entirely wrong when applied to the script because it appeared in the Hittite cultural sphere, but the language written with it was Luwian, not Hittite. Italian scholars denote the script 'Anatolian Hieroglyphic' after the geographical area in which it occurs rather than the language written with it. This approach has the advantage of not having to attribute the still unclear origins of the script to the Luwians.

📖 *The Luwians*: Melchert, 2003, esp. 1–2; Bryce, 1998, 14–16; 54–55; *Language Family*: Bryce, 1998, 10–11; Carruba, 1998, 270; Crossland and Birchall, 1974; Makkay, 1993; Melchert, 1994, 11–12; 2003, 170–171; 2003, 23–26; Oettinger, 2002b, 50–55; Yakubovich, 2010a, esp. 18–90. *Terminology*: Marazzi, 1990, 19–22; Hawkins, 2000, 1.

1.1.2   Hieroglyphic Inscriptions

The Hittite Empire with its capital city Hattusa (modern Boğazköy) dominated large areas of Anatolia and North Syria from the 17th to 13th century BC. The state archives preserve many thousand clay tablets which were inscribed with the cuneiform script and in several languages, chiefly the official language Hittite, further Akkadian, the *lingua franca* of the Ancient Near East, and predominantly in cultic context, Hurrian. Further, Cuneiform texts also record the Luwian language at Hattusa; these are mainly confined to ritual texts of the 16th-15th century BC and Luwian loanwords in Hittite texts. The appearance of a second writing system at a time when cuneiform already provided a suitable writing medium is remarkable. The rise of this second script seems to have been connected to Hittite royal self-representation. With the exception of digraphic seals, the two scripts, cuneiform and hieroglyphic, were never used together.

Early pictorial symbols are attested in Anatolia from the 18th century BC onwards but seem to have recorded messages rather than words and cannot be connected with a particular language or with the hieroglyphic script as used during the Hittite Empire period. The earliest systematic usage of the hieroglyphic script appears on Hittite official and royal seals after 1500 BC, recording names and titles of the seal owners. Epigraphs and inscriptions are attested from the time of Muwatalli II onwards. The oldest dateable inscription remains ALEPPO 1, an inscription of Talmi-Šarruma; previously, the ANKARA silver bowl has been considered as the earliest inscription (time of Tudhaliya I/II) but it can now be firmly dated to the 12th century BC.[1] The four longer Bronze Age inscriptions are to be dated to the Late Hittite Empire, in particular to the time of the last two great kings, Tudhaliya IV and Suppiluliuma II. Comparison with the later inscriptions of the Iron Age shows that these Bronze Age texts record an earlier stage in the development of the hieroglyphic script. A few hieroglyphs of this period are no longer in use after the end of the Bronze Age, while other signs with double values can be seen to develop into two differentiated signs, e.g. *zi/a* separates into *zi* and *za*. Another characteristic of the period is the predominance of logographic writings and the infrequent use of nominal and verbal endings. Both limit our knowledge of vocabulary and grammatical structure of these inscriptions.

The transition from Bronze to Iron Age was accompanied by major political changes. The Hittite Empire disintegrated about 1200 BC and the fall of its capital Hattusa brought an end not only to the central administration but also to cuneiform writing in the Hittite territories in Anatolia and North-Syria. Several smaller centres of political power emerged, some of them in important cities of the Hittite Empire. Karkamiš, for instance, once the seat of the Hittite viceroy and in direct control of the Syrian territories, shows no signs of disruption and

---

1   Payne, forthcoming.

continues to hold a position of power for several more centuries. The so-called 'Neo-Hittite States' in many ways preserved the Hittite legacy and cultural traditions. They used Hieroglyphic Luwian as their sole writing system, causing the script to flourish. While one should not conclude that Luwian had therefore become the only spoken language, the preserved personal names from the period suggest that a majority of the population may have been Luwian speaking. The Iron Age inscriptions comprise the largest part of the Hieroglyphic corpus and are commonly divided into ten groups according to their Neo-Hittite state of origin, namely Cilicia, Karkamiš, Tell Ahmar, Maraş, Malatya, Commagene, Amuq, Aleppo, Hama and Tabal. The texts are conventionally named after their find spot and in the case of several inscriptions from one location also numbered. The extant hieroglyphic corpus consists to the largest part of stone inscriptions, the extreme durability of the material having insured their survival. But writing on stone was a laborious task deemed appropriate only for certain texts. The surviving corpus therefore mainly preserves the literary genres of building, dedicatory and commemorative inscriptions. The few surviving examples of hieroglyphic writing on metal, meanwhile, attest a much wider usage of the script, and for different types of literature; extant are for instance business letters and economic documents on lead strips. Unfortunately, the scarcity of such documents and the lack of comparable data severely limit our understanding of the vocabulary involved, and therefore of the texts. We may postulate a lost text corpus which took place on perishable materials such as wood, papyrus or leather, and valuable, re-usable materials such as metal, but one can only speculate as to its extent and content. The script is regarded as fully developed by the time it records particle chains, nominal and verbal endings and shows greater tendency towards phonetic rather than logographic spelling, c. 1000 BC. It is in use until about 700 BC, when most Neo-Hittite states lost their independence.

Many open questions remain: By whom, why, when and where was the script invented? Are there attributable outside influences? What is the relationship between the Hittites and hieroglyphic writing? And why is it confined to Luwian? At present, the origins of the hieroglyphic script remain very much obscure.

📖 *Historical Background:* Bryce, 2012; 2003, 27–127; Hawkins, 1982, 372–441; 2000, 38–45, 73–79, 224–226, 249–252, 282–288, 330–333, 361–365, 388–391, 398–403, 425–433; 2002; 2003, 148–151; Jasink, 1995; Mazzoni, 1982, 1994; Mora–d'Alfonso 2012; *Origins and Development of the Script:* Mora, 1991, 1994, 1995; Hawkins, 2003, 166–169; Carruba, 1998. Payne, forthcoming; *Iron Age Inscriptions:* Hawkins, 2000, 19–21; 2003. *Online Map of inscriptions:* http://www.hittitemonuments.com/

1.2   The Script

1.2.1   Writing Materials and Appearance

The hieroglyphic script is mainly preserved on stone monuments but also on
seals and seal impressions, and in a few cases on other materials such as a piece
of shell, pottery and metal. As mentioned above, it is probable that hieroglyphic
writing had also been used on other perishable materials but one can only
speculate about the extent of this usage and the techniques employed. The stone
monuments take various shapes, ranging from rock reliefs to building blocks,
stelae, and carved figures, mainly lions. The most common types of stone were
basalt and limestone in various colours.

To date, there is little evidence on scribes and scribal schools, although the
range of local styles seem to argue for the existence of local schools. Stone
inscriptions were fashioned in one of two ways, either by cutting away the
background thus leaving the writing in relief, or by incising the signs on the
smooth surface. 'Writing' on stone was predictably a mason's task, but it
remains unknown whether the mason was a specialized scribe himself or
worked according to a scribal draft, possibly drawn onto the stone.

As regards the sign forms, one differentiates between a more elaborate
monumental and a more abstract linear or cursive form. These sign forms are
neither mutually exclusive nor confined to a particular time and place, and
indeed sometimes interchange in a single word. But as a general trend, relief
inscriptions commonly use monumental sign forms while incised ones prefer
the linear version. In later periods there seems to have been a tendency towards
incised inscriptions. The hieroglyphic script may be written in either direction,
and texts of several lines generally run *boustrophedon* 'as the ox ploughs', i.e.
alternating from line to line. Lines were divided by horizontal rulings. The
direction of writing can be determined with the help of the non-symmetrical
signs which always face the beginning of the line.[2] Within a line signs are
generally written in vertical columns but occasionally aesthetic considerations
take precedence over the placement of signs, thereby obscuring the correct
reading order.

📖 Hawkins, 2000, 4; 2003, 155–156, 161–162.

---

2   But beware of the 'foot' (*90/*93) which may face either way.

1.2.2   The Signs

The hieroglyphic script consists of over 500 signs, some with multiple values, which function as 1) logograms, 2) determinatives, and 3) syllabograms, or a combination thereof. Series of signs sharing the same value, whether logographic or syllabic, are numbered beginning with the most frequent sign, thus e.g. NEG, NEG$_2$, NEG$_3$, or *sa*, *sá* (*sa$_2$*), *sà* (*sa$_3$*), *sa$_4$*, *sa$_5$*. The general principles of transliteration will be indicated under the respective sign types. All signs are accorded a number based on Laroche's sign list,[3] commonly quoted as L.No. or *No. Look at the following sign with logographic and syllabic value:

☛   *90   PES   ti

☞ The foot, number ninety, has the logographic value PES, 'foot' and represents the syllable *ti*.

1.2.2.1   Logograms

The signary contains some 225 logograms which represent a word or concept with one sign, and can sometimes be understood by their pictorial character. The underlying Luwian word is not always known to us, and you may find logograms transcribed in older publications with Sumerian words or the native language of the scholar. However, it is now conventional to transcribe logograms with Latin terms and in capitals. Only two abbreviations are used, REL for the relative, and NEG for the negative, and a very small number of Logograms are accorded their Luwian equivalent, transcribed with cursive capitals. Logograms of unknown meaning are referred to by their number only. Compare the following:

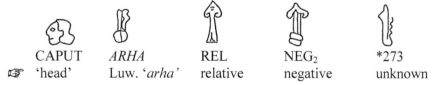

CAPUT	*ARHA*	REL	NEG$_2$	*273
☞ 'head'	Luw. '*arha*'	relative	negative	unknown

1.2.2.2   Determinatives

Logograms are sometimes used to classify a noun or verb as belonging to a specific group, and are either placed before or after the word concerned.

---

3 Laroche, 1960b.

Determinatives are transliterated in brackets (except for the personal marker ¹),
and, as logograms, in capitals. Commonly pre-determined are for instance
personal and god names, while geographic names tend to be post-determined.

(DEUS)	¹	(REGIO)	(URBS)
god	person	country	city

1.2.2.3 Syllabograms

Syllabograms are the signs used to write the language phonetically. They stand
for simple vowels (*V*) and in combination with consonants (*C*) for syllables of
the structure *CV*, less frequently *CVCV*. Few signs show a different structure;
they are mainly confined to the Empire period. Some signs have several
vocalisation options and are transliterated with a dash, e.g. *wa/i* (*wa* or *wi*),
la/i/u (*la, li* or *lu*). While the origins of many syllabic values are still unknown,
some syllabograms can be analysed as derived by acrophony, i.e. the first
syllable of a depicted word is used as the syllabic value of the sign. Thus the
picture of the giving hand *66 (luw. *piya*- 'to give') has the syllabic value *pi*.

a	*mu*	*hara/i*
V	*CV*	*CVCV*

1.2.2.4 Words

Words may be written with a logogram, a logogram with phonetic complements
or a full phonetic writing; not infrequently logogram and full phonetic writing
are used together, the logogram acting as a determinative. Look at the following
examples for the Luwian word for 'fortress':

CASTRUM	CASTRUM-*sà*	(CASTRUM)*ha+ra/i-ní-sà*
log.	log. + phon. compl.	log. + full phon. writing

Purely phoentic spellings also occur but the step to abolish logographic writing
in their favour was never taken. If it is unclear whether the phonetic spelling

following a logogram represents the complete word or not, a hyphen in brackets connects logogram and phonetic spelling: LOGOGRAM(-)*phonetic writing*. Occasionally, syllabograms are added as phoentic indicators to logograms, the consonant of the syllable representing a consonant of the stem of the underlying word. Phonetic indicators are transliterated in cursive capitals; cf. below, 2.2.

📖 Hawkins, 1986, 363ff; Melchert, 1996, 120–124; *Sign lists*, see below, 1.3.2.2.

1.3   Research

1.3.1   The Story of Decipherment

The story of decipherment begins in the 19th century AD, ante-dating even the rediscovery of the Hittites. As early as 1812, the Swiss scholar J.L. Burckhardt saw stone blocks covered with unknown hieroglyphs in the Syrian city of Hama. The coming decades brought to light an increasing number of such hieroglyphic inscriptions in both Syria and Anatolia, while the recently deciphered Egyptian hieroglyphic and Babylonian cuneiform texts attested a powerful Hittite empire in this region. The connection was made when A.H. Sayce in a lecture in 1876 claimed that the Hama writing was Hittite. By the beginning of the 20th century AD, L. Messerschmidt published a corpus of hieroglyphic inscriptions, comprising a total of 32 major and 29 minor texts, as well as a collection of seals and epigraphs.[4] Early decipherment attempts, however, achieved little beyond the identification of some logograms. Not surprisingly, as both script and language of the texts were unknown. At the time there was no bilingual other than the problematic digraphic TARKONDEMOS seal.

This unpromising situation began to change with H. Winckler's excavation at Boğazköy in 1906, which unearthed the Hittite capital Hattusa, including archives with more than ten thousand cuneiform tablets, written in several languages. The cuneiform script, which had been deciphered in the second half of the 19th century AD, and the large number of Akkadian texts were instantly readable and provided some information on the Hittites. The decipherment of the other main tongue, the official language of the Hittite Empire, was quickly achieved with surprising results: Hittite was an Indo-European language, as were Luwian and Palaic, also recorded on these tablets albeit much less frequently. The knowledge of these early Anatolian languages provided the linguistic background for the decipherment of the hieroglyphic inscriptions.

---

4   Messerschmidt, 1900; 1902; 1906.

Meanwhile the hieroglyphic corpus continued to grow, especially since the 1911-1914 excavations in Karkamiš on the Euphrates and in near-by Tell Ahmar in 1929-1931 provided numerous inscriptions. From Boğazköy came around 200 seal impressions,[5] among them some digraphic ones in hieroglyphic and cuneiform, providing mini-bilinguals, and others in hieroglyphic only. Decipherment experienced its first successes during the 1930s at the hands of five scholars, working separately on the available material, namely P. Meriggi, I. Gelb, E. Forrer, H.Th. Bossert and B. Hrozný.[6] Their achievements include the correct interpretation of many logograms and syllabograms, and a sketch of the grammar. Erroneous identifications, on the other hand, rendered these results still unreliable. The language of the inscriptions was identified as closely related to but different from both Hittite and Luwian, its exact position within the Anatolian language family still being debated.

In 1946, Bossert and H. Çambel discovered a long bilingual inscription in Karatepe. The text, written in Hieroglyphic and Phoenician, survived in a pair of duplicates and provides seventy-five closely parallel clauses, still the longest Hieroglyphic inscription to date. Although the final publication only appeared in 1999,[7] preliminary versions were available and the text confirmed many hypothetical readings, established new ones and increased the knowledge of the language and vocabulary. It failed, however, to induce some necessary corrections of misinterpretations. The same can be said for further digraphic seal impressions found at Ugarit in 1953 and 1954.

It was a French scholar, E. Laroche, who correctly identified the language as a Luwian dialect, and in 1960 published a systematic sign list which still provides the basis of our modern sign lists.[8] Designated 'first part', a grammar and text editions were intended to follow it. Important research tools were also published by Meriggi, who published a glossary and a corpus of inscriptions which included the large number of new texts and remained the chief tool for over a quarter of a century. Meanwhile several articles, especially by Mittelberger and Bossert, began to question the reading of certain signs, and the discovery of Urartian pithoi in Altıntepe with measures written in Hieroglyphic provided new material for a re-evaluation of some incorrect readings.[9]

In 1973,[10] J.D. Hawkins, A. Morpurgo Davies and G. Neumann postulated a number of 'new readings' which have since been generally accepted and, because of affecting some common syllabic signs, have changed the

---

5 Published by Güterbock, 1940, 1942.
6 Meriggi, 1933, 1934a, 1934b; Gelb, 1931, 1935, 1942; Forrer, 1932; Bossert, 1932; Hrozný, 1933, 1934, 1937.
7 Çambel, 1999.
8 Laroche, 1957/1958, 160; 1960b.
9 Mittelberger 1962, 1963, 1964; Bossert, 1960, 1961a, 1961b.
10 Published 1974.

reconstruction of the language considerably. The paper further affirmed Laroche's identification of the language as Luwian. In recent years various publications have added to the available reference tools for the study of Luwian, both Cuneiform and Hieroglyphic, and have brought the two much closer together. To name only the most important, since 1990 have appeared an extensive study of the stem formation of Luwian nouns,[11] a collection of literature on Hieroglyphic Luwian with signary,[12] a lexicon of Cuneiform Luwian,[13] the final publication of the KARATEPE bilingual as part of a new corpus of Hieroglyphic Luwian inscriptions of the Iron Age[14] and the corpus itself,[15] and a volume on the Luwians.[16] Most recent additions include three volumes on seals,[17] a socio-economic history of the Neo-Hittite states,[18] a socio-linguistic study of the Luwian language,[19] three Festschriften with relevant articles[20] and a political history of the Neo-Hittite states.[21] A corpus of the Bronze Age hieroglyphic inscriptions with signary, grammar and glossary is in preparation,[22] and a new conference volume entitled "Luwian identities" should appear shortly.[23] New text finds and further insightful research keep this field of study a very dynamic discipline and promise an exciting future.

📖   J. Friedrich, 1939, 1954; J.D. Hawkins, 2000, 6-17; 2003, 130–138; Payne, 2003. *New Readings*: Hawkins, Morpurgo Davies and Neumann, 1974; Rieken–Yakubovich 2010; Simon 2008; Yakubovich 2010a: 81–8.

1.3.2   Research Tools

Unfortunately, the use of the available research tools still poses some serious problems, particularly to beginners. The subject is still a comparatively young and dynamic discipline, and in the past decades many new results have been achieved, as illustrated above. Much of the available and relevant source material is therefore partly, and to complicate matters in varying ways out-dated. To be able to use the reference material, it is necessary to understand

---

11 Starke, 1990.
12 Marazzi, 1990.
13 Melchert, 1993.
14 Çambel, 1999.
15 Hawkins 2000.
16 Melchert 2003.
17 Herbordt 2005; Dinçol and Dinçol 2008; Herbordt, Bawanypeck and Hawkins 2011.
18 Giusfredi 2010.
19 Yakubovich 2010a.
20 Penney 2004; Kim et al. 2010; Singer 2010.
21 Bryce 2012.
22 Hawkins, forthcoming.
23 Mounton, Rutherford and Yakubovich 2013.

which stages and systems of research the publication in question reflects, and how to 'translate' its results to the current standard.

1.3.2.1   Text Editions

Most Iron Age inscriptions can now be found in *CHLI* with full bibliography, photo and drawing, transliteration, translation and commentary. For a list of Bronze Age inscriptions see Hawkins, 2003. As noted above, the reading of individual hieroglyphs has changed over the years, particularly after the new readings of 1973/4. Publications prior to this date must be read with the relevant changes in mind.[24]

📖 Hawkins, 2000; 2003, 139–140; Meriggi, 1966, 1967, 1975, 1975a; Hrozný, 1933, 1934, 1937; Charles, 1911; Messerschmidt, 1900, 1902, 1906. *Online bibliography of Bronze Age inscriptions*: http://luwianforum.blogspot.com; *Online bibliography of newly found Iron Age inscriptions*: http://agyagpap.blogspot.com/2010/10/list-of-iron-age-luwian-inscriptions.html

1.3.2.2   Sign Lists

The most up-to-date sign lists are published by Marazzi. The earlier publication is restricted to Iron Age signs with extensive bibliographical references. The second volume, the Acts of the Procida Round Table, represents the current state of research and includes both Bronze and Iron Age signs. For signs of uncertain value one must still consult the partly out-dated Laroche. Note that the sign lists of Laroche and Meriggi adopt different numbering systems - conversion tables are given in both publications. Most scholars nowadays use a modified version of Laroche's sign list but a few, notably Poetto, still follow Meriggi. The sign list in this book provides drawings of all signs, other than abandoned Laroche numbers, with current values.

📖 Laroche 1960; Marazzi, 1990, 1998; Meriggi, 1962; *Sign Tables:* Hawkins, 2000, 26–27, 29, 33; Hawkins apud Herbordt, 2005, 397–436. *Conversion tables*: Laroche, 1960b, 269–284; Meriggi, 1962, 240–241. *New Readings*: Hawkins, Morpurgo Davies and Neumann, 1974, 50, table 1; Rieken–Yakubovich 2010; Simon 2008; Yakubovich 2010a: 81–83.

---

24 Compare e.g. Hawkins, Morpurgo Davies and Neumann, 1974, 50, table 1.

1.3.2.3   Dictionaries

The only dictionary is provided by Meriggi, a publication which poses two problems: for the hieroglyphs it adopts a numbering system no longer used, and because of the publication date it cannot reflect the new readings. Marazzi provides a lexical list with bibliographical references but without translations. *CHLI* contains an index of words discussed, by their nature problematic rather than simple words. Because of the topic of his study, the list of words discussed by Starke is equally limited. Melchert's Cuneiform Luwian Lexicon can be used for reference but the differences between the Cuneiform and Hieroglyphic text corpora apply not only to literary genre but also to vocabulary involved. The vocabulary section of this book will provide all words needed for the sample texts as well as a selection of further important words, hopefully a useful tool for further reading. Work on a Luwian dictionary is in progress.[25]

📖   Hawkins, 2000, 625–636; Melchert, 1993; Meriggi, 1962; Marazzi, 1990, 375–402, Starke, 1990.

1.3.2.4   Grammars

Many articles have been published on grammatical topics, but there are few comprehensive grammars dedicated specifically to the study of Hieroglyphic Luwian. Most recently, see Melchert's discussion of the Luwian languages. On nominal formation, see also Starke. Marazzi provides an introduction to the grammar with bibliographical references to the relevant articles. For a comparative Anatolian grammar, see Meriggi. The grammar section of this book tries to give a necessarily brief overview of phonology, morphology and syntax with references to selected articles.

📖   Marazzi, 1990, 50–82; Melchert, 2003, 170–210; Meriggi, 1980, 1953; Starke, 1990.

---

25 Yakubovich, forthcoming.

2   Phonology

The following sections aim to introduce the main grammatical features. References to secondary literature are selective and have been chosen to include only the most important, comprehensible and up-to-date treatments. This volume can only provide a short introduction to signs, sounds and the main phonological rules. For more in-depth treatments refer to the literature quoted.

📖   Melchert, 1994; 2003, 177–185.

2.1   Signs and Sounds

1. The script represents the vowels *a, i, u,* and the following consonants, conventionally rendered as *h, k, l, m, n, p, r, s, t, w, y, z.*
2. Signs have the structure V or CV, less often CVCV (cf. 1.2.2.3). A few signs, mainly from the Empire period, show a different structure.
3. Two signs show dual vocalisation *(ra/i, wa/i)*, one triple *(la/i/u)*.
4. Some sounds can be expressed with several signs (homophones). To differentiate homophone signs, they are numbered according to frequency. The most frequent value, no. 1, bears no mark (e.g. *sa*), no. 2 carries an acute accent over the vowel (*sá*), no. 3 a grave (*sà*), no.s 4 onwards an index number (*sa₄*). Common doublets include *a/á, ha/há, ni/ní, nu/nú*. With five common variants, the *sa-* and *ta*-series have the largest number of homophones. Note that the *ta*-signs are only interchangeable within the groups ta_{1-2} and ta_{3-5}, see below 2.3.
5. For a discussion of the different sign types (logograms, determinatives and syllabograms) and principles of transliteration cf. above, 1.2.2.

The table on the following page shows the most frequent phonetic signs. The three double columns of the regular syllabary show the signs on the left, their phonetic value on the right, and below it its number according to Laroche, 1960b. For the signs *u, mu, ma, sà* and *ta*, both monumental and cursive shapes are given as they differ greatly.

2.2　The Regular Syllabary

	a (450)		*i* (209)		*u* (105)
	á (19)		*ia* (210)		
	ha (215)		*hi* (413)		*hu* (307)
	há (196)				
	ka (434)		*ki* (446)		*ku* (423)
	la (176)		*li* (278)		*la/i/u* (445)
	ma (110)		*mi* (391)		*mu* (107)
	na (35)		*ni* (411)		*nu* (153)
			ní (214)		*nú* (214)
	pa (334)		*pi* (66)		*pu* (328)
	ra/i (383)				*ru* (412)
	sa (415)		*si* (174)		*su* (370)
	sá (433)				
	sà (104)				
	sa₄ (402)				
	sa₅ (327)				
	ta (100)		*ti* (90)		*tu* (89)
	tá (29)				*tú* (325)
	tà (41)				
	ta/i₄ (319)				
	ta/i₅ (172)				
	wa/i (439)				
	za (377)		*zi* (376)		*za₅* (432)

A few remarks on certain common signs:

1. The sign *19 *á* is only used word-initially.
2. The sign *450 *a* can be subject to two different graphic practices, s. below 2.3 and 2.5.
3. The sign *391 *mi*, sometimes written in ligature with logograms, frequently acts as a phonetic indicator, signalling the presence of an *m* in the stem of the word represented by the logogram. Most commonly, it occurs with AEDIFICARE (*tama-*, 'to build'), AUDIRE (**tuma(n)ti-*, 'to hear') and OMNIS (*tanima/i-*, 'all, every').
4. A few other syllabograms are used as phonetic indicators to provide a word's first syllable, for instance in the personal name MONS.*TU*, 'Tudhaliya' or the word for son, INFANS.*NI*, '*nimuwiza-*.
5. The enclitic sign *383 *ra/i* is always attached to the preceding sign, transliterated +*ra/i*. In contrast, *a*+*ra/i* and *i*+*ra/i* - unless word-initial - are understood to define the vocalisation of the sign *ra/i* and follow it in transliteration, thus *ra*+*a* representing /ra/, *ri*+*i* representing /ri/, e.g.[26]

|*ha-tu*+*ra/i-* [27]   *ha-ri*+*i-ti* |*ha-tu-ra*+*a*

The sign *ra/i* is also involved in most CVCV signs (*tara/i* etc.).

2.3   Graphic Representation of Sounds

1. There is no clear indication of vowel length. Double ('plene') writing of vowels may indicate length but also occurs in positions where the second vowel is interpreted as marking the end of a word (cf. below, 2.5.).
2. Consonant clusters or word-final consonants cannot be expressed with this syllabary. Since there are no signs for single consonants, syllables with superfluous vowels have to be written instead. In such cases, generally the *a*-series is used, e.g. writing –*sa* for -*s* (n.sg.C.).
3. Preconsonantal *n* is hardly ever written, leaving for instance the ending of the 3.pl.prt. -*nta* indistinguishable from the singular form -*ta*, e.g. *a-za-ta* could represent both *azata* 'he loved' and *azanta* 'they loved'. However,

---

26 Excerpts from ASSUR letter *e*, §§ 3; 1; 4.
27 For the transliteration of the last sign cf. below, 2.5.

there is one criterion of distinction: Rhotacism (s. below, 2.4) can only occur intervocalically, and therefore only affects the 3.sg.

4. A peculiar graphic practice affects the simple vowel sign *450 *a* when in word-initial position. Bronze Age inscriptions and seals show that scribes frequently displaced the sign, writing it at the end rather than at the beginning of a word. This practice is now seen to extend into the Iron Age, with an added difficulty: notably later texts omit the sign altogether - maybe the scribes no longer understood that the sign was dislocated and thought it superfluous.[28] The writing of initial-*a*-final is indicated in transliteration with an asterisk. Thus *wa/i-ma-tá-*a* stands for /*a=wa=mu=ata*/ (KARKAMIŠ A11b+c, § 10) while *wa/i-mu* represents /(*a)=wa=mu*/ (MARAŞ 1, § 2). For a different usage of the sign, s. below, 2.5.

5. Tenues (*k, p, t*) and mediae (*g, b, d*) are not differentiated. But as noted above, the homophones *ta*$_{1-2}$ are not interchangeable with *ta*$_{3-5}$ which may indicate a differentiation between *ta* and *da*.

📖 Carruba, 1984; Hawkins, 2003, 159–161; Hawkins, Morpurgo Davies and Neumann, 1974, esp. 166; Melchert 1987; 2003, 177–185, 182; 209–10; Rieken, 2008.

2.4   Phonological Rules

1. *Rhotacism:*
Hieroglyphic Luwian shows a tendency to replace an intervocalic voiced dental with the letter *r*, a feature called rhotacism. It particularly affects the enclitic personal pronoun *-ata/-ara*, the abl. sg./pl. *-ati/-ari*, and the 3.sg.prs *-ti/-ri*, 3.sg.prt. *- ta/-ra* and 3.sg.imp. *-tu/-ru*.

2. *Deletion:*
a) Word final stops are deleted, also if followed by the neuter particle *-sa/-za*, e.g. *mamu(t)*-, 'partner' loses its stop in the nominative *ma-mu-sa(-ha)* (ASSUR letter *f+g*, § 1) but retains it in the oblique cases, cf. the dative *ma-mu-ti(-ha)* (ASSUR letter *f+g*, § 1). We only have attestations for final dental stops.
b) Deletion of word initial *a* (*aphaeresis*) is also common. But differentiate the merely graphic omission of word-initial *a-* in the cases described above, 2.3.
c) Syncope may affect the suffixes *-iya- > -i-* and *-uwa- > -u-*.

📖 Friedrich, 1958; Morpurgo Davies, 1982/83; Melchert 2003, 172–173, 179–182.

---

28 Cf. Hawkins 2003, 159–161.

2.5   Reading Aids

If a text has several lines, they are normally separated by line-dividers. They are not represented in transliteration but the end of a line is marked with two vertical lines (‖). The script contains certain signs which may serve the modern reader as reading aids, although they are by no means used consistently. Thus signs *450 *a*, and rarely *209 *i*, experience secondary usage marking the end of a word, possibly originally used as a space filler. This is transliterated as shown below.

Sign	Transliteration	Function
ଠଓ	¦[29]	indicates the beginning of a word
ଛଓ	" "	marks a hieroglyph as a logogram
𒀼	-ʾ	may indicate the end of a word/be used as a space filler
𒀺	-*i*	may indicate the end of a word/be used as a space filler

----

29 Notably Meriggi and Poetto, also Starke, 1990, transliterate k instead of ¦.

3 Morphology

Because of the restricted nature of the hieroglyphic text corpus not all grammatical forms are attested.

3.1 The Noun

3.1.1 Formation

3.1.1.1 Suffixes

The most productive suffixes are:
1. Abstract nouns are formed with the following suffixes:
   a) *-ahit-*: *hantahit-*, 'pre-eminence', e.g. |"FRONS"-*hi-ti* (KARKAMIŠ A15b, § 14),
   b) *-astra/i-*: *sanawastra/i-*, 'goodness', e.g. |("BONUS")*sa-na-wa/i-sa-tara/i-ti* (KARATEPE 1, § XVIII, Hu.).
2. Animative suffixes originally enabled inanimate words to become the subject of a sentence. The animative suffix *–ant-* occurs e.g. in *tipasant(i)-* 'heaven' (BOYBEYPINARI 2 § 21).
3. *Nomina instrumenti* are formed with the suffixes:
   a) *-ut(i)-*: *arut(i)-*, 'basket(?)', e.g. ("*78")*a-ru-ti-zi* (ASSUR letter *a*, § 10),
   b) *-al-*: *huhurpal-*, 'part of war chariot' e.g., ("LIGNUM")*hu-hú+ra/i-pa-li* (KARKAMIŠ A11b+c, § 10).
4. Professional titles are formed with the suffixes:
   a) *-za-*: *kumaza-*, 'priest', e.g. |*ku-ma-za-sa-pa-wá/i-na*[... (KAYSERİ, § 17),
   b) *-ala/i-*: **tapariyala/i-*, 'governor', e.g. |LEPUS+*ra/i-ia-li-i-sa* (MARAŞ 1, § 1b).
5. Feminine forms of prominent masculine terms end in *-s(a)ra/i-*: *nanasra/i-* 'sister', e.g. (FEMINA)*na-na-sa₅+ra/i-za-ha* (MARAŞ 6, 1.1); cf. also the Hittite loan word *hasusara-* 'queen', e.g. (FEMINA)*ha-su-sa₅+ra/i-sa* (KULULU 5, § 7b).
6. Neuter words can be formed with the suffixes:
   a) *-tar-*: *iziyat(a)ra-*, 'ritual', e.g. |*i-zi-ia-tara/i-za-'* (MARAŞ 14, § 7),
   b) *-man-* (*nomina actionis* from verbs): *saman-* 'sealed document(?)', e.g. |*sà-ma-za* (KULULU 2, § 2).
7. Deverbal nouns can be formed with the suffixes
   a) *-sha-*: *niyasha-* 'procession' < *(ni)niya-* 'to follow', e.g. CRUS.CRUS(-)*ní-ia-sa-ha-na* (KARKAMIŠ A11b+c, § 16),

b) *-ma/i-*: *sama/i-* 'shooting' < *sa-* 'to press, seal; shoot', e.g. |*sà-ma-ia* (BOHÇA § 5).

8. Derived adjectives end in:

   a) *-iya-* (often contracted to *-i-*): *tatiya-*, 'paternal', e.g. |*tá-ti-ia-za* (TELL AHMAR 2, § 3), and *tati-*, 'paternal', e.g. |*tá-ti-i* (KARATEPE 1, § XVI, Hu.),

   b) *-ala/i-*: *warpala/i-*, 'brave', e.g. ("SCALPRUM+*RA/I.LA/I/U*") *wa/i+ra/i-pa-li-sa* (MARAŞ 1, § 1d),

   c) *-il(i)-*: *antatili-*, 'interior', e.g. *a-tá-ti-li-i-sa* (BABYLON 1, § 11).

9. Relics of an *-ant*-participle form are preserved as lexicalized adjectives, e.g. *walant(i)-*, 'dead' (KUB 35.45 ii 26; KUB 35.48 ii 20).

10. The suffix *-ala/i-* expresses belonging to: *irhala/i-*, 'frontier-post', e.g. FINES+*RA/I*+*HA-ha-li* (TOPADA, §).

11. The suffix *-want-* denotes provision with: *waliyawant-*, 'full of exultation(?)', e.g. |*wa/i-li²-ia-wa/i-ti-na* (KULULU 4, § 9).

12. Possession is denoted most commonly with the suffix *-asa/i-* ('genitival' or 'possessive' adjective): *Warpalawa/isa/i-*, 'of Warpalawas', e.g. |*wa/i+ra/i-pa-la-wa/i-si-sa* ... SERVUS-*ta₄-sa*, 'servant of Warpalawas' (BULGARMADEN, § 1); less frequently with the suffix *–iya-*: REGIO-*ni(-)*DOMINUS-*ia-i-sa*, 'of the Country-Lord' (KARKAMIŠ A1b § 1).

📖 Melchert, 1990, 202f.; 2003, 195–199; Plöchl, 2003, 52–61; Starke, 1990.

3.1.1.2 Compound Nouns

Hieroglyphic Luwian appears to have a few compound nouns which consist of two nominal elements only the latter of which takes case endings. Examples include REGIO-*ni(-)*DOMINUS 'country-lord' (e.g. KARKAMIŠ A2+3, § 1) and DOMUS-*ni(-)*DOMINUS 'house-lord' (e.g. KULULU 4, § 8).

📖 Melchert, 2003, 198–199.

3.1.2 Inflection

3.1.2.1 Categories

Nouns and adjectives show gender, number and case. Hieroglyphic Luwian shows:

a) two genders, common (animate) and neuter (inanimate),

b) two numbers, singular and plural (collective and count),

c) five cases, nominative, genitive, dative-locative, accusative, and ablative-instrumental.[30] Instead of a vocative, the forms of the nominative are used. As expected, in both singular and plural the neuter has one form for nominative and accusative. In the plural, also the common gender has only one form for nominative and accusative.

3.1.2.2 Endings

Nouns and adjectives take the following endings:

Case Endings				
	Singular		Plural	
N.c.	*-s*	**N/A.c.**	*-nzi*
A.c.	*-(a)n*		
N./A.n.	*-n, -Ø*	**N/A.n.**	*-a(ya)*
G.	*-(a)s, -(a)si*		
D.	*-i(ya), -a, -an*	**D.**	*-anza*
Abl.	*-ati*	**Abl.**	*-ati*

Some remarks on the case endings:
a) As the hieroglyphic script cannot write final consonants, the nominative ending *-s* is written with the *sa*-series (sa_{1-8}).
b) The nominative-accusative singular neuter is commonly followed by a particle *-sa/-za.*
c) In the singular, the inherited genitive competes with the possessive adjective; in the plural, only the possessive adjective is used. This denominal adjective, formed with the suffix *-asa/i-,* inflects in agreement (of case, number and gender) with its subordinate noun. It cannot express plurality of its base noun.
d) The dative in *-an* is confined to possessive adjectives in *-asi-.* The form was presumably developed to avoid confusion with the ordinary genitive ending *-asi.*
e) Because the hieroglyphic script cannot write final consonants, the accusative common ending *-n* is generally written with the sign *na*, occasionally with NEG$_2$ (*ná*).
f) The ablative does not show number.

📖 *Cases*: Marazzi, 1990, 62–65; Melchert, 2003, 186–187; Meriggi, 1980, 275–316; Morpurgo Davies, 1980a; Starke, 1982; 1990; *Neuter particle*

---

30 Abbreviated in the following N. (nominative), G. (genitive), D. (dative-locative), A. (accusative), Abl. (ablative-instrumental).

-*sa*/-*za*: Arbeitman, 1977; Carruba, 1982; van den Hout, 1984; Melchert, 2003, 186. *Possessive Adjective*: Melchert, 2003, 186; 188; Neumann, 1982.

3.1.2.3   *i*-Mutation

A peculiar feature of the nominal inflection is the so-called '*i*-mutation' (also '*i*-Motion', although strictly speaking the phenomenon should not be called a motion because it does not involve change of gender).

Many nouns insert an obligatory -*i*- between stem and case ending in the nominative and accusative forms of the common gender, singular and plural, thereby obscuring the original stem. *A*-stems delete their stem vowel before mutation-*i*, thus showing a mixed paradigm of forms with -*a*- and -*i*-. A further complication that occurs is *a*-mutation or 'reverse *i*-mutation', when original *i*-stems treat their stem vowel as if derived by *i*-mutation and begin replacing it with an -*a*-.

Many instances of *i*-mutation are obscured by the hieroglyphic script as a number of syllabograms do not distinguish between *a* and *i*. Depending on how many forms of a word are attested, it may or may not be possible to discern its original stem.

Hoffner and Melchert, 2007, 86–87; Melchert, 2003, 187–188; Oettinger, 1987, 35–43; Plöchl, 2003, 42–44; Rieken, 1994, esp. 43 n.6.; Starke, 1990, 86ff.

3.1.2.4   Examples

Because most nouns are attested in only few cases, a few examples must suffice as an illustration. Not attested forms are indicated with an asterisk.

Sg.	*huha*- 'grandfather'	Pl.	
N.c.	*huhas*	N/A.c.	*huhanzi*
A.c.	*huhan*		
G.	**huhas(i)*		
D.	*huha*	D.	**huhanza*
Abl.	*huhati*	Abl.	**huhati*

Sg.	*tata/i-* 'father'	Pl.	
N.c.	*tatis, taris*	**N/A.c.**	*tatinzi*
A.c.	*tatin*		
G.	**tatas(i)*		
D.	*tati*	**D.**	*taranza, *tatanza*
Abl.	**tatati*	**Abl.**	**tatati*

Sg.	*tati(ya)-* 'paternal'	Pl.	
N.c.	**tatis*	**N/A.c.**	*tatinzi*
A.c.	**tatin*		
N/A.n.	*tatiyan-za*	**N/A.n.**	*tatiya*
G.	**tati(ya)s*		
D.	*tati*	**D.**	**tatiyanza*
Abl.	**tatiyati*	**Abl.**	**tatiyati*

Sg.	**kuwalan-* 'army'	Pl.	
N/A.n.	**kuwalan-za*	**N/A.n.**	**kuwalana*
G.	**kuwalanas*		
D.	**kuwalani*	**D.**	**kuwalanza*
Abl.	**kuwalanati*	**Abl.**	**kuwalanati*

3.1.2.5 Comparison

Evidence for a morphological comparative is sparse and superlative forms are not known at all. One can tentatively identify a comparative suffix *-(t)ara/i* in forms such as POST+*ra/i-* (*apara/i-*) 'later' and INFRA-*ta+ra/i-* (**anantara/i-*) 'lower', e.g. POST+*ra/i-zi-pa-wa/i-tú* |FRATER-*la-zi-i* 'his younger brothers' (KARKAMIŠ A15b, § 15).

For syntactical means of comparison, s. 4.2.3 and 4.3.

3.2 The Pronoun

3.2.1 Personal Pronouns

Orthotonic pronouns of the 1st and 2nd Person			
1.sg. 'I'	2.sg. 'you'	1.pl. 'we'	2.pl. 'you'
N. *amu* (EGO)	*ti*	*anzanz(a)*	*unzanz(a)*, *unzans(a)*
D. *amu*	*tu*		
A. *amu*	*tu*		
Abl.	*tuwati*?		*unzati*? *(u-za-ri+i, u-za+ra/i-i)*

a) The 1st singular *amu* occurs also as *mu* due to loss of its initial *a* (aphaeresis).
b) The ablatives *tuwati* and *unzati rhotacise to *tuwari*, *unzari*; it is not entirely clear whether these forms belong to the personal or possessive pronoun (or both).
c) The third person uses the demonstrative *apa-* as its personal pronoun.
d) For the reading of the sign *432 *za₅* and the spread of dative forms of the 1st and 2nd plural to the nominative s. Yakubovich.
e) Hieroglyphic Luwian commonly uses orthotonic pronouns together with the corresponding enclitic forms, s. below 4.6.

📖 Marazzi, 1990, 66; Morpurgo Davies, 1980b, 89; Oshiro, 2000, 189–193; Yakubovich 2010a: 79–83.

3.2.2 Enclitic Forms

The 1st and 2nd person have the following enclitic forms. There appears to be no differentiation of case.

Enclitic Pronouns of the 1st and 2nd Person			
1.sg.	**2.sg.**	**1.pl.**	**2.pl.**
'I'	**'you'**	**'we'**	**'you'**

	1.sg.	2.sg.	1.pl.	2.pl.
N./D./A.	*-mu*	*-tu, -ti(?)*	*-anza*	*-manza*

The third person distinguishes case, using the following forms:

Enclitic Pronouns of the 3rd Person		
	3.sg.	**3.pl.**
N.c.	*-as*	*-ata*
A.c.	*-an*	*-ata*
N./A.n.	*-ata*	*-ata*
D.	*-tu*	*-manza*

a) The forms *-tu, -ti, -ata* also appear rhotacised as *-ru, -ri, -ara.*
b) If attached to a word or particle ending in *-a*, it is impossible to distinguish between the enclitic pronoun *-ata* and the locative particle *-ta* other than through context.

📖 Morpurgo Davies, 1980b, 89–90 and n.9.

3.2.3 Reflexive Pronouns

The reflexive pronoun is attested in the following enclitic forms:

1.sg	2.sg	3.sg	1.pl.	2.pl.	3.pl.
-mi	*-ti*	*-ti*	*-anza*	*-manza*	*-manza*

a) There are seven attestations of an element *-si* being added to what appears to be a perfectly good verbal ending: *hwihwisa(n)ta-si* (KARKAMIŠ A11b+c § 8; A12 § 2), *huhasata-si* (TELL AHMAR 6 §§ 7, 17), *iziha-si* (ALEPPO 2 § 8), *iziya-si* (ÇINEKÖY, §§ 6, 7). These forms have been alternatively explained as medio-passives or, as seems more likely, as active verbs with a reflexive pronoun *-si.*

📖 Meriggi, 1980, 319; Morpurgo Davies, 1980b, 89; Oshiro, 1983; Rieken, 2004.

3.2.4   Possessive Pronouns

The possessive pronouns are *ama/i-*, 'my', *tuwa/i-*, 'your' (2.sg.), *anza/i-*, 'our' and *unza/i-*, 'your' (2.pl.). The following forms are attested:

Singular	1.sg.	2.sg.	1.pl.	2.pl.
N.c.	*amis*	*tuwis*	*anzis*	*unzis*
A.c.	*amin*	*tuwin*		*unzin*
N./A.n.	*ama(n)-za*			
D.	*ami*			
Abl.	*amiyati*	*tuwati?*	*anziyati*	*unzati?*

Plural	1.sg.	2.sg.	1.pl.	2.pl.
N./A.c.	*aminzi*			
N./A.n.	*ama*		*anzaya*	
D.	*amiyanza*			

a) The third person singular and plural uses the possessive adjective of the demonstrative *apa-*, e.g. *apasi-* / *pasi-* (aphaeresis).
b) The first singular *ami-* also occurs as *mi-* (aphaeresis).

📖   Carruba, 1986; Meriggi, 1980, 320–321.

3.2.5   Demonstrative Pronouns

Hieroglyphic Luwian has two demonstratives, *za-*, 'this' and *apa-*, 'that'. The latter also functions as the orthotonic personal pronoun of the 3rd person, s. 3.2.1. The following forms are attested:

	Singular			Plural	
N.c.	*zas*	*apas, apis*	N./A.c.	*zanzi*	*apanzi, apinzi*
A.c.	*zan*	*apan, apin*	N./A.n.	*zaya*	*apaya*
N./A.n.	*za*	*apa*	D.	*zat(iy)anza*	*apatanza*
G.	*zas(i)*	*apas(i)*			
D.	*zati*	*apati*			
Abl.	*zin*	*apin*			

a) The demonstrative and relative (cf. 3.2.6) pronouns add a dental suffix to the stem in the dative-locative singular and plural which seems to derive from an Indo-European locative suffix *-dhe.[31]

b) Several adverbs are derived from the demonstratives: *apati* 'there', *zati* 'here'.

📖 Goedegebuure, 2008; Melchert, 2003, 190–191; Meriggi, 1980, 322–323.

3.2.6 Interrogative and Relative Pronouns

The stem *kwi-/kwa-*, written with the logogram REL, is used as interrogative and relative pronoun. The following forms are attested:

	Singular		**Plural**
N.c.	*kwis*	**N./A.c.**	*kwinzi*
A.c.	*kwin*	**N./A.n.**	*kwaya*
N./A.n.	*kwa(n)-za*	**D.**	*kwatanza*
D.	*kwati*		
Abl.	**kwati*		

a) For the dental suffix of the dative, s. 3.2.5.

b) A general relative 'whosoever, whatsoever' is formed through either reduplication (*kwis kwis,* also *kwis ima kwis*) or conjunction with the indefinite pronoun *kwis-ha*.

c) Two adverbs are derived from the relative *kwitan* (REL-*ta-na*) 'where, wherever (to)' and *kwipa* (REL-*pa*) 'indeed; so'.

d) Several conjunctions derive from the relative: *kwari* (REL+*ra/i*) 'because, since; as, as if, like; if; when', *kwati* (REL*(-a)-ti*) 'if; (so) that; wherefore; when(?)', *kwa(n)za* (REL-*za*) 'since, because; why; even though'; *kwi* (REL-*i*) 'even though; when, while'.[32]

📖 Hawkins and Morpurgo Davies, 1993; Oshiro, 1983.

3.2.7 Indefinite Pronouns

Relative pronoun plus a suffix *-ha* serves as indefinite pronoun, *kwis-ha* 'someone', $NEG_{(1-3)}$ *kwis-ha* 'no one'.

---

31 Cf. Schmidt, 1988, 225.
32 The status of the various derivates from the relative is not entirely clear yet.

	Singular		Plural
N.c.	*kwis-ha*	**N./A.c.**	*kwinzi-ha*
A.c.	*kwin-ha*	**N./A.n.**	*kwaya-ha*
N./A.n.	*kwa(n)-za-ha*	**D.**	**kwatanza-ha*
D.	*kwati-ha*		
Abl.	**kwati-ha*		

3.3   Numerals

Only very few Luwian words denoting number are known since most attestations consist of numeral signs with or without case endings. One would expect a system of cardinal and ordinal numbers, as well as expressions of multiplication and fraction.

a) Only three words for cardinals are attested: *tuwa/i-* 'two', *tari-* 'three' and *nu(wi)(n)za-* 'nine'.

b) Ordinals appear to be formed with a suffix *-ti-*, cf. 1-*ti-na* 'first(?)' (ASSUR letter *b*, § 4).

c) Multiplication appears to be expressed through either a suffix *-su*, cf. "4"-*su* 'four times(?)' (KARKAMIŠ A6, § 19) or a suffix *-ta*, cf. 9-*ta* 'nine times(?)' (HİSARÇIK 1, §§ 2, 4).

d) Fraction appears to be expressed through a suffix *-ti/-ta*, cf. 9-*ti-sa-ha-wa/i-ti⌈-i?⌉* 'ninth(?)' (HİSARÇIK 1, § 3), *ti-na-ta-za* 'tenth(?)' (SULTANHAN, § 28).

📖 Carruba, 1979; Meriggi, 1980, 328–330; Plöchl, 2003, 99.

3.3.1   Numeral Signs

The script attests an extensive decimal system with signs representing one (|), ten (−), one-hundred (5) and one-thousand (<). The numerals signs are combined in two ways, most commonly in an additive fashion beginning with the highest units followed by the smaller ones, and occasionally in multiplication, smaller unit preceding the higher, compare

42 (40+2),   100,   151 (100+50+1),   200 (100+100),

but   100 (1x100).

3.4 The Verb

3.4.1 Formation

3.4.1.1 Suffixes

The most productive suffixes are
a) -sa- (iterative), compare |pi-pa-sa-i 'he always gives' (BOHÇA, § 3) and |pi-ⁱ⌈a⌉-a-i 'he gives' (KULULU 1, § 14),
b) -za- (iterative), compare *ARHA*[?!] ("CRUSˇ⁾")ta-za-tu, 'let it continue to stand' (KARATEPE 1, § LXXIV) and CRUS-ia (taya), 'he shall stand' (CEKKE, § 22),
c) -nu(wa)- (causative), compare (SOLIUM)á-sa-tá 'they sat' (KARKAMIŠ A11b+c, § 10) and (SOLIUM)i-sà-nú-wa/i-ha 'I seated' (KARKAMIŠ A11b+c, § 17).

3.4.1.2 Reduplication

Reduplication occurs in the present and past tense and has iterative force, compare (LIBARE)sa₅+ra/i-la-i-ti 'they will offer' (ANCOZ 1, § 2) and sa-sa₅+ra/i-la-ti, 'they shall always offer' (MARAŞ 5, § 2); pi-ya-ta, 'she gave' (KARKAMIŠ A23, § 5) and pi-pa-sa-ta, 'she always gave' (KARKAMIŠ A23, § 4).

3.4.1.3 Preverbs

Verbs are frequently modified by one or several preverbs. The most common are:
a) *anan (SUB-na-na) 'under': |("PES")pa+ra/i-za |SUB-na-na |tu-wa/i-ta, 'he put under (his) feet' (SULTANHAN, § 9),
b) anta (a-ta) 'in, inside': a-ta tu-pi-wa/i, 'I shall incise' (KARATEPE 1, § LXX, Hu.),
c) antan (a-ta-na) 'in, into': a-ta-na PES₂.PES₂-ti, 'they will come in' (KARKAMIŠ A31+, § 8),
d) apan(i) (a-pa-na, POST-ni/-na) 'behind, after': |POST-ní || |PES-wa/i-ta, 'they came after (me)' (KARKAMIŠ A11a, § 15); |POST-ni |SOLIUM-nu-wa/i-ha, 'I re-established' (KARKAMIŠ A23, § 10),
e) arha (ARHA) 'forth', also denotes intensity, 'completely': |ARHA |i-wa/i, 'I shall go away' (KULULU 1, § 15); ARHA |tà-ia, 'he shall take away' (KARKAMIŠ A6, § 27); |ARHA |á-za-tu, 'may it eat up' (KULULU 1, § 12),

f) CUM-*ni/-i* '?': [BONUS-*za*(?)] ⌈NEG₂⌉ CUM-*ni i-zi-i-ti*, 'he shall not do good' (KARKAMIŠ A31+, § 13),

g) *kata (INFRA-*ta*) 'down': INFRA-*ta-ha-wa/i-ta* ‖ |("PES")*u-sá-ha*, 'and I brought them down' (KARATEPE 1, § XXIX, Hu.),

h) *paran(i)* (PRAE-*na/-ni*) 'before, in front of': |*á-mu* ‖ REL-*zi* |PRAE-*na* |*á-sá-ta*, 'who were before me' (KARATEPE 1, § XXVII, Hu.),

i) *pari* (PRAE-*i*) 'over': |PRAE-*i pi-ia-ha*, 'I gave (it) over' (BABYLON 1, § 9),

j) *sara* (SUPER+*ra/i*) 'up, over': |SUPER+*ra/i* |"PES"-*wa/i+ra/i,* 'he shall come up' (SULTANHAN, § 30).

3.4.2   Inflection

3.4.2.1   Categories

Hieroglyphic Luwian has one verbal conjugation, comparable to the Hittite -*mi*-conjugation, and very few traces of a second (-*hi*-)conjugation. Because of the nature of the text corpus, some verbal forms are poorly or not at all documented. Hieroglyphic Luwian distinguishes between:

a) two voices, active and medio-passive,
b) two tenses, present and preterite,
c) two moods, indicative and imperative,
d) a verbal noun,
e) an infinitive,
f) a gerundive,
g) a participle.

3.4.2.2   Verbal Endings

	Present Indicative		Preterite Indicative	
	act.	**med.-pass.**	**act.**	**med.-pass.**
1.sg	-*wi*		-*ha*	-*hasi*
2.	-*si* [-*tis*]		-*ta*	
3.	-*ti* / -*ri*, [-*i*, -*ia*]	-*ati* / -*ari*	-*ta*	-*asi*, -*tasi*
1.pl			-*han(?)*	
2.	-*tani*		-*tan*	
3.	-*nti*		-*nta*	-*antasi*

	Imperative	
1.sg.		
2.	-∅	
3.	-tu	-aru
1.pl.		
2.	-ranu <*-tanu	
3.	-ntu	

Participle
-am(m)a/i-

Verbal Noun	-ur-
Infinitive	-una
Gerundive	-min(a)

a) Less frequent endings are given in square brackets.
b) The following forms rhotacise: 3.sg.ind. -ti / -ri, 2.pl.ind. -tani / -rani, 2.pl.imp. *-tanu / -ranu.
c) For an alternative explanation of -han as a nasalised 1.sg.prt. see Carruba.
d) For the alleged medio-passive ending -si, cf. 3.2.3.
e) The participle does not show voice.
f) For a gerundive in -min(a) (previously identified as 1.pl.prs.) see Melchert, 2004.

📖 Carruba, 1984; Meriggi, 1980, 330–366; Melchert, 2003, 191–194; 2004; Morpurgo Davies, 1979, 577–610; 1980, 86–108; 1982/83, 245–269; Oshiro, 1993; Rieken, 2004; Starke, 1979, 247ff.; Tekoğlu, 2000, 980.

3.4.2.3 Examples

Most verbs are only attested with a few forms. The common verb *izi(ya)-* 'to make' is attested in the following forms:

Prs.ind.act.: 1.sg. *iziwi* (KARATEPE 1, § LXIX, Hu.), *iziyawi* (ASSUR letter *e*, § 9), 3.sg. *iziti* (KÖT˜KALE, § 6), *iziri* (KULULU 5, § 4), *iziyati* (BULGARMADEN, § 10), *iziyari* (TEKİRDERBENT 1, l. 4), 1.pl. *iziyamin* (CEKKE, § 10); Prs.ind.med.-pass.: 3.sg. *iziyati* (ANCOZ 7, § 3), *iziyari* (MARAŞ 14, § 5); Prt.ind.act.: 1.sg. *iziha* (KARATEPE 1, § VIII, Hu./Ho.), *iziyaha* (MARAŞ 3, § 3), 3.sg. *izita* (KARATEPE 1, § III, Hu.), *iziyata* (HAMA 6, § 3), 3.pl. *iziyanta* (KARABURUN, § 5); Imp.act.: 3.sg. *izitu* (IZGIN 2, § 9), *iziyatu* (KULULU 1, § 11), 3.pl. *iziyantu* (CEKKE, § 28); Imp.med.-pass.: 3.sg. *iziyaru* (KARATEPE 1, § L, Ho./Hu.).

4   Syntax

4.1   Agreement

1. Adjectives agree in case, number and gender with the noun they qualify.
2. Attributes to possessive adjectives in -*asi*- agree in case, number and gender with the adjective they qualify and do not themselves express possession through either the genitive or the suffix -*asi*-.
3. The verb agrees in number with the subject. If a sentence has more than one subject or a plural subject expressing a single concept or if the subject is a neuter plural, the verb may be either singular or plural.
4. Present indicative and imperative forms of the verb *as*- 'to be' are frequently omitted (nominal sentences).
   a) (ind.): EGO-*wa/i-mi* ^{I}*ru-wa/i-sa* 'I (am) Ruwas' (KULULU 1, § 1)
   b) (imp.): [|]*sa-pi-su+ra/i-wa/i-a-ti* 'health (be) to you' (ASSUR letter *e*, § 2).
5. Cardinal numbers greater than one and nouns in agreement with them may be either singular or plural.

4.2   Use of Cases

4.2.1   Nominative

The nominative is the case of the subject and of predicate nouns and adjectives (*who? what?*): EGO ^{I}*ka-tu-wa/i-sa* |"IUDEX"-*sa kar-ka-mi-si-za-sa*(REGIO) REGIO DOMINUS-*ia-sa* 'I (am) Katuwas the ruler, the Karkamišean Country-Lord' (KARKAMIŠ A2+3, § 1).

4.2.2   Genitive

The genitive is the case of the complement and expresses belonging of a person or thing to another (*whose? whereof?*): *mu-ka-sa-sá-há-*' DOMUS-*ní-...*, '... the house of Muksas' (KARATEPE 1, § LVIII, Hu.).

Luwian can replace the possessive genitive with a possessive adjective, e.g. 'the gods of the father' could either be expressed with the genitive (**tatis masaninzi*, 'the gods of the father'), or the noun could be qualified with a possessive adjective, usually in –*asa/i*- (**tatasinzi masaninzi*) but sometimes in -*iya/i*- (**tatinzi masaninzi*), 'paternal gods, gods of the father'. Neither adjective can express plurality of its base noun.

4.2.3   Dative-Locative

Hieroglyphic Luwian has but one case for the dative, denoting the indirect object (*to whom? for whom?*) and the locative (*where?*). The dative-locative is used as the case of

a) interest (*to whom? for whom?*): *za-pa-wa/i* ("STELE")*wa/i-ni-za* (DEUS)*pa-ha-la-ti-ia* CRUS-*nu-ha-á*, 'and this stele I set up for Ba'alat' (RESTAN, § 3),

b) aim (*to what end? what for?*): |*u-za₅-za*||-*wa/i-ma-za* |*ha-tu-ra+a*, 'you yourselves (are) for writing, i.e. you must write' (ASSUR letter *a*, § 4).

c) location (*where?*): ("CASTRUM")*ha+ra/i-ní-sà-pa-wá/í* |PUGNUS(-)*la/i/u-mi-tà-ia*⌈AEDIFICARE⌉-*MI-ha* |("FINES")*i+ra/i-há-za*, 'And I built strong fortresses on the frontiers' (KARATEPE 1, § XIX, Hu.+Ho.),

d) direction (*where to?*): *pa-tá-za-pa-wa/i-ta-'* (TERRA+*LA*+*LA*)*wa/i-li-li-tà-za mi-i-zi-'* |*tá-ti-i-zi* AVUS-*ha-ti-zi-ha* |*348(-)la/i/u-tà-li-zi-ha* |NEG₂-*'* (PES₂)*HWI-HWI-sà-tá-si*, 'My fathers, grandfathers and ancestors had not marched to those fields' (KARKAMIŠ A11b+c, § 8),

e) possession (*whose?*): *wa/i-ti-'* ... |*á-ta₅-ma-za i-zi-i-sa-ta-i*, 'he honours the name for himself, i.e. his own name' (KARKAMIŠ A1b, § 2),

f) comparison: *pa-sa-za-*⌈*pa²*⌉-*wa/i-mu-'* |FRATER-*la-za* MAGNUS+*ra/i-za-na* |*i-zi-i-tà,* 'He made me great(er) than his brothers' (TELL AHMAR 1, § 16).

g) time (*when?*): *...á*]-*ma-za* |("STATUA")*tá-ru-sa pa-ti-i-'* |(ANNUS)*u-si* |CRUS-*nu-wa/i-*[*ha*], 'I set up my statue in that year' (KARKAMIŠ A25a, § 7),

h) object of an infinitive: REL-*pa-wa/i-mu* POST-*na* |(DEUS)TONITRUS-*hu-za-sá* (DEUS)CERVUS₂-*za-sá-há* |*sá-ta za-ti* "CASTRUM"-*si* AEDIFICARE-*mi-na,* 'so Tarhunzas and Runzas were after me for this castle to build (it)' (KARATEPE 1, § XL, Hu.).

i) respect(?): |*u-sa-ta-mu-ti-sà-ha-wa/i-'* |*ha-tu+ra/i-'* 'You are falling(?) in error(?) as regards writing! (ASSUR letter *e*, § 3).

4.2.4   Accusative

The accusative is the case of the direct object (*whom? what?*) of transitive verbs. The accusative further expresses

a) σχῆμα καθ' ὅλον καὶ μέρος: |*á-mu-pa-wa/i-na* |*za-ti* (MANUS)*i-sà*||-*tara/i-na* |*tà-ha,* 'here I took him by the hand' (KARKAMIŠ A7, § 3),

b) extent of time: POST-*na-wa/i* ARHA^{?!} ("CRUS<">)*ta-za-tu* |*ara/i-zi* OMNIS-*MI-zi* (OCULUS)*á-za-ti-wa/i-tà-sa* |*á-ta₅-ma-za* 'hereafter may the name Azatiwatas continue to stand for all ages' (KARATEPE 1, § LXXIV, Hu.); *a-wa/i* |TONITRUS-*hu-na-*(LITUUS)*á-za-sa-za-'* DEUS-*na-za*

|"OVIS"-*ru-pi* |*sa₅-sa₅+ra/i-la-i* |"ANNUS"-*na* ANNUS-*na*, 'and he shall offer year by year a *kurupi*-sheep to the gods of Tarhunzas' (BULGARMADEN, § 11).

The verb *iziya*- 'to make' takes a double accusative of direct and indirect object: *wa/i-mu-u* (DEUS)TONITRUS-*hu-za-sa á-TANA-wa/i-*||*ia*(URBS) MATER-*na-tí-na tá-ti-ha i-zi-i-tà*, 'and Tarhunzas made me mother and father for Adanawa' (KARATEPE 1, § III, Hu.).

4.2.5 Ablative-Instrumental

Hieroglyphic Luwian has one case for the ablative (*whence?*) and the instrumental (*wherewith?*). It is the case of

a) separation (*where from? from what?*): REX-*ta-ti-i-pa-wa/i* ... REL-*sa-ha*, 'anyone from (among) the kings' (KARATEPE 1, § LIX, Hu.).

b) place of origin (*where from?*): *wa/i-tu-tá-'* || CORNU+*RA/I-ti*(REGIO) |LIS *ARHA* SPHINX, 'against him arose a quarrel from the land Sura' (KARKAMIŠ A4b, § 2).

c) instrument (*wherewith? by what means?*): |*wa/i-na* |("ANNUS")*u-si-na* |("ANNUS")*u-si-na* 1 ("BOS.ANIMAL")*wa/i-wa/i-ti-i* 3 ("OVIS. ANIMAL")*ha-wa/i-ti* |*sa-sa₅+ra/i-la-wa/i*, 'and I shall sacrifice (to) him year by year with an ox (and) three sheep' (KULULU 1, § 6); ... *kar-ka-mi-si-za-sa*(URBS) MAGNUS.DOMINA-*sa₅+ra/i-sa* "MANUS"-*ti* |PUGNUS-*ta*, 'the Queen of Karkamiš raised (me) by the hand' (KARKAMIŠ A23, § 3).

d) cause (*why?*): *wa/i-mu-' mi-i-sa-'* DOMINUS-*na-ni* || (DEUS)TONITRUS-*sa* (DEUS)*kar-hu-ha-sa* (DEUS)*ku+AVIS-pa-sa-ha mi-ia-ti-'* |"IUSTITIA"-*na-ti* (LITTUS)*á-za-ta*, 'and because of my justice my lord Tarhunzas, Karhuhas and Kubabas loved me' (KARKAMIŠ A11a, § 7),

e) agent of a passive participle: DEUS-*na-ti* (LITUUS)*á-za-mi-sà* ... REX-*ti-sá*, 'the king loved by the gods' (MARAŞ 1 § 1h).

4.3 Comparison

Comparison is mainly expressed by syntactical means (but cf. 3.1.2.5).

a) Adjectives following FRONS-*la/i/u* = *hantili*- 'foremost' may represent comparatives, e.g. |FRONS-*la/i/u* ARGENTUM.DARE-*si-ia* 'foremost in cost = very costly(?)' (KARKAMIŠ A11a, § 17).

b) The comparative dative may be used: *noun₁* - *noun₂* (dat.) - *adj.* (agreeing with noun 1) '*noun₁* is more *adj.* than *noun₂*': *pa-sa-za-⌈pa?⌉-wa/i-mu-'* |FRATER-*la-za* MAGNUS+*ra/i-za-na* |*i-zi-i-tà,* 'he made me great(er) than his brothers' (TELL AHMAR 1, § 16); cf. 4.2.3.

4.4   Adverbs

Hieroglyphic Luwian has local (*where?*), temporal (*when?*) and modal (*how?*) adverbs. Adverbs can be derived from adjectives by using the nominative and accusative singular or plural of the neuter adjective, e.g. *wasu*: |*w*[*a/i-s*]*u-u* || *u-sa-nu-sá-ha*, 'I benefited well' (BULGARMADEN, § 8); *wala*: [*wa/i*]-*tú-tá-*' (DEUS)*á-tara/i-su-ha-sa* |("CRUX")*wa/i-la/i/u* |PES-*wa/i-tú*, 'against him may Atrisuhas come fatally' (KARKAMIŠ A4d, § 2). For adverbs derived from pronouns s. above, 3.2.5, 3.2.6.

4.5   Postpositions

Hieroglyphic Luwian has postpositions,[33] many of which also function as pre- and adverbs. Case alone can express certain syntactical relationships for which English needs prepositions, e.g. Dative 'in', Ablative 'from, out of'.

Most postpositions take the dative:
a) *anan* (SUB-*na-na*) 'under': ("PES")*pa-tà-za* |SUB-*na-na*, 'under the feet' (KARATEPE 1, § XXII, Hu.),
b) *anta* (*a-ta*) 'in': REGIO-*ni-i a-tá*, 'in the country' (KARKAMIŠ A2+3, § 7),
c) *apan(i)* (*á-pa-na*, POST-*na/-ni*) 'behind, after': REL-*pa-wa/i-mu* POST-*na*, 'and so after me' (KARATEPE 1, § XL, Hu.),
d) CUM-*na/-ni* 'together with': *wa/i-na-*' ¹MAGNUS+*ra/i*-TONITRUS-*tá-sa-za* |INFANS.NEPOS-*sa-za* CUM-*ní*, 'him together with the grandsons of Ura-Tarhunzas' (KARKAMIŠ A11b+c, § 4),
e) *hanti* (FRONS-*ti*) 'in front of, before': *ta-ni-mi-i-ha-a-wa/i* || DEUS-*ni-i*, 'and in front of every god' (KARKAMIŠ A6, § 20),
f) *kumapi* 'together with(?)': (DEUS)*ku+AVIS-ia ku-ma-pi*, 'together with(?) Kubaba' (KARABURUN, §§ 8, 10),
g) *paran(i)* (PRAE-*na/-ni*) 'before, in front of': *wa/i-tú-wa/i-na-*' |PRAE-*na*, 'and it before him' (KARKAMIŠ A12, § 13),
h) *pari* (PRAE-*i*) 'before, at': |"PODIUM"-*ta-ti* PRAE-*i*, 'at the podium' (KARKAMIŠ A1a, § 20),
i) PRAE-*ti* (*par(iy)a(n)ti(?)* / *hanti(?)*) 'before': DOMINUS-*ti-wa/i+ra/i-ia-pa-wa/i á-ha-li-sa-na* PRAE-*ti*, 'before DOMINUS-tiwaras (son) of Ahalis' (CEKKE, § 12),

---

33 Except for: |CUM-*ha-wa/i-tú*, 'with him' (KARKAMIŠ A1a, § 27); |PRAE-*wa/i* |*á-mu*, 'before me' (ASSUR letters e § 31); |PRAE-*pa-wa/i-za-ta*, 'before us' (ASSUR letters f+g § 30).

j) *sara* (SUPER+*ra/i*) 'over, above': *kar-ka-mi-sà*(URBS) SUPER+*ra/i*, 'over Karkamiš' (KARKAMIŠ A15b, § 2),

k) *sara(n)ta* (SUPER+*ra/i-ta*) 'upon, over': (EQUUS.ANIMAL)*zú-na* (EQUUS)*zú-wa/i* |SUPER+*ra/i-ta,* 'horse upon horse' (ÇİNEKÖY, § 4); OMNIS-*MI-za* |REX-*ta-za* SUPER+*ra/i-ta,* 'over all kings' (KARATEPE 1, § LII, Ho.),

l) *tawiyan(i)* (VERSUS-*na/-ni*) 'towards': ORIENS-*mi* VERSUS-*na,* 'towards the east' (KARATEPE 1, § XXX, Hu./Ho.)

m) *336-na-na* 'in the sight of(?)': |DEUS-*na-za* |CAPUT-*tá-za-ha* |*366-na-na,* 'in the sight(?) of gods and men (KARKAMIŠ A2+3, § 24).

One postpositions takes the ablative:

a) *arha* (*ARHA*) '(away) from': CAELUM-*ti ARHA,* 'from the sky' (TELL AHMAR 2, § 19).

📖 Plöchl, 2003, 74–83; Poetto, 1979.

4.6 Pronouns

1. For the order of enclitic pronouns in particle chains, s. 4.11.
2. Since verbal forms already contain the person of the subject, additional use of orthotonic pronouns indicates emphasis.
3. Sentences with the verb 'to be', including nominal sentences, whose subject is in the first or second person require use of the appropriate reflexive pronoun. It may or may not be accompanied by the orthotonic pronoun.

4.7 Verbs

4.7.1 Voices

The active voice denotes that the action of the verb proceeds from the subject. The medio-passive voice denotes either that the action proceeds from and benefits the subject (medium) or that the subject is the recipient of the action (passive). Passive action is mainly expressed with the passive participle.

4.7.2 Tenses

1. The tenses do not differentiate aspect.
2. The present is used for
   a) the present: ... |*á-ta$_5$-ma-za i-zi-i-sa-ta-i,* 'he honours the name' (KARKAMIŠ A1b, § 2),

b) the future: ... *á-ta₅-ma-za ARHA* MALLEUS-*i*, 'he shall erase the name' (KARKAMIŠ A11a, § 25)

c) the past (historical present): |*á-mi-zi-pa-wa/i* |*tá-ti-zi-i* |AVUS-*ha-zi-ha* |REL-*zi* [|?]*sa-ta* |REL-*pa-wa/i* (DEUS)TONITRUS-*hu-za-sa* |NEG₂ |REL-*ha-na* |*wa/i+ra/i-ia-ia*, 'and (those) who were my fathers and grandfathers, indeed Tarhunzas did not help (them) at all' (BOHÇA, §§ 6-7).

3. The preterite is used

a) for all past tenses: NEG₂-*ha-wa/i-sa mi-i-' AVUS-ha* POST-*ni a-tá* |BONUS-*li-ia*||-*ta wa/i-sa-' mu-' ka-tu-wa/i-ia kar<-ka>-mi-si-za*(URBS) REGIO(-)DOMINUS-*ia* "COR"-*tara/i-na* POST-*ni a-tá* BONUS-*li-ia-ta*, 'for my grandfather he had not exalted (the person) but for me, Katuwas, the Kar(ka)miˌsean Country-Lord, he exalted the person' (KARKAMIŠ A2+3, §§ 4-5),

b) to express state: [*ARHA*]-⌈*pa-wa/i*⌉-*sá* |REL-*i* ("MORI")*wa/i-la-tá wa/i-mu-' pa-si-i-'* |(INFANS)*ni-mu-wa/i-i-za-sa* MALUS-*wa/i-z*⌈*a*⌉-' CUM-*ni* |("LIGNUM")LEPUS+*ra/i-ia-ta*, 'but when he died (i.e. now that he was dead), his son decreed evil for me (TELL AHMAR 1, §§ 18-19).

4.7.3   Moods

1. The indicative is used

a) for factual statements: *wa/i-mu⁻ⁱ* |*á-ma-*⌈*z*⌉*a* ("STELE")*wa/i-ni-za* "CRUS"-*nu-wa/i-ha*, 'and I set up my stele' (MARAŞ 14, § 4).

b) for the iussive (indicative present): |*mu-pa-wa/i-ta-'* ... *i-zi-i-sa-ta-i*, 'he shall also honour mine' (KARKAMIŠ A1b, § 2).

2. The imperative is used for order as well as wishes: |(LOQUI)*ta-tara/i-ia-mi-sa i-zi-a-ru*, 'let him be made accursed' (KARKAMIŠ A2+3, § 24).

3. A negative command (prohibitive) is expressed with *ni(s)* (NEG₃) and the indicative present: |NEG₃-*sa* |LITUUS+*na-ti-i*, 'let him not behold' (KARKAMIŠ A2+3, § 23); a few late examples use the imperative instead (e.g. ASSUR letter e § 13).

4.7.4   Verbal Nouns

1. The verbal noun in -*ur* inflects and is used as a noun.

2. The expression verbal noun + *as*- 'to be' denotes obligation: |*wa/i-ma-za* |*u-za₅-za* |*ha-tu-ra+a* |*a-sa-ta-ni*, 'you yourselves are for writing, i.e. you are to write' (ASSUR letter *e*, § 6).

3. The infinitive is always dependent on a main verb or predicate.

4. The expression 'infinitive + *ta*- 'to step' means 'to begin to do something':
   wa/i-na |i-zi-sa-tu-na ta-ia ("FLUMEN")*há-pa+ra/i-sá* |OMNIS-*MI-sá* ...,
   'every river-land will begin to honour him' (KARATEPE 1, § XLVIII, Hu.).
5. The gerundive expresses obligation and is used predicatively with the verb
   as- 'to be'.
6. Participles are nominal forms and inflect as nouns.

4.8   Word Order

1. The verb commonly stands at the end of the sentence.
2. The subject frequently precedes the object. Sentences are commonly
   introduced by a conjunction with added particle chain (cf. 4.11.).
3. Other subordinating conjunctions are normally found within the sentence.
4. The relative pronoun frequently follows the subject.
5. Interrogative pronouns are usually placed sentence-initially.
6. The position of the negative within the sentence is relatively free. It
   commonly precedes the verb (and its preverb) or the relative and indefinite
   pronoun to form expression like NEG$_2$ REL-*sa-ha* 'no one' (cf.3.2.7).

4.9   Negatives

1. Negative statements are expressed with *na(wa)* (NEG$_2$) and the indicative:
   |REL-*pa-wa/i* (DEUS)TONITRUS-*hu-za-sa* |NEG$_2$ |REL-*ha-na* |*wa/i+ra/i-
   ia-ia*, 'indeed Tarhunzas did not help at all' (BOHÇA, § 7).
2. Prohibitions are expressed with *ni(s)* (NEG$_3$) and the indicative: |NEG$_3$-*sa*
   |LITUUS+*na-ti-i,* 'let him not behold' (KARKAMIŠ A2+3, § 23).
3. Double negatives occur either with negative adverbs or to reinforce
   prohibitive statements: |*a-ta-pa-wa/i-na* |*ni-i-i* |*ma-ru-ha* |*pa-nu-wa/i-i*
   |TONITRUS-*hu-za-sa* |*tu-wa/i+ra/i-sa*, 'may Tarhunzas by no means let
   him *drink* in the vineyard' (SULTANHAN, § 36); |*ni-wa/i-mu^i* |*á-pi* |NEG$_2$-'
   |VIA-*wa/i-ni-si*, 'Don't not send (them) back to me!' (ASSUR letter *d*, § 10).

📖 Hawkins, 1975.

4.10   Questions

Questions can be identified either through context or the use of interrogative
pronouns, e.g. *ni-pa-wa/i-na* |*á-mu* |REL-*za* |*i-zi-ia-wa/i* |*á-mi-na* |*za-na* |*ha-
tu+ra/i-na*, 'or why do I make it, this letter of mine?' (ASSUR letter *e*, § 9).

4.11 Particles

Hieroglyphic Luwian sentences are generally introduced by a particle chain consisting of various enclitic particles added to the first accented word of the sentence. While not all possible elements need be used, the order in which the various particles are added to one another is fixed:

1. conjunction *a-*, orthotonic pronoun or any other accented word,
2. connective particle *-pa* 'but' or *-ha* 'and',
3. quotative particle *-wa,*
4. enclitic pronouns (dative forms preceding nominative and accusative forms),
5. locative particle *-ta.*

☞ If attached to a word or particle ending in *-a*, the local particle and the third person enclitic pronoun *-(a)ta* look similar but as has recently been demonstrated, the pronoun is spelled with *tà* while the particle is spelled with *ta* or *tá.*

📖　Carruba, 1985; Rieken, 2008.

4.11.1　Quotative Particle

The particle *-wa* indicates quoted speech. As written documents were generally intended to be read out, it is omnipresent. It is untranslatable.

4.11.2　Locative Particle

The locative particle *-ta* is used especially with verbs of motion or expressions of direction and location. It is untranslatable.

4.11.3　Connective Particles

1. In particle chains, the adversative *-pa* and the connective *-ha* are mutually exclusive.
2. To join two words, the connective *-ha* is added to the second element, e.g. |*tá-ti-zi-i* AVUS-*ha-zi-ha,* 'fathers and grandfathers' (BOHÇA § 6).
3. Connection is frequently expressed without connective particles (asyndeton).

4.11.4　Disjunctive Particles

There are two disjunctive particles, *nipa* 'or' and *napa* 'or' which both consist of a negative (*ni-/na-*) plus connective particle (*-pa*).

📖　Morpurgo Davies, 1975.

4.12 Subordinate Clauses

Subordinate clauses can be identified through their use of subordinating conjunctions, usually placed within or even at the end of the subordinate clause. All subordinate clauses are dependent on a principal clause. Coordination of clauses is altogether more frequent than subordination.

4.12.1 Causal Clauses

Causal conjunctions include *kwari* (REL+*ra/i*) 'because', *kwanza* (REL-*za*) 'because' and *kuman* 'because', the verb stands in the present or preterite indicative: |NEG$_2$-*wa/i-na* |REL+*ra/i-i* (LOCUS)*pi-ta-ha-li-ia-ha*, 'because I did not *exile* it' (KARKAMIŠ A11b+c, § 31); "LIGNUM"-*sa-pa*||-*wa/i-mu-tá-'* |REL-*a-za za-a-ti-ia-za* |(DOMUS.SUPER)*ha+ra/i-sà-tá-na-za* POST-*ni* |PES-*wa/i-tà*, 'because wood came after me for these *upper floors*' (KARKAMIŠ A11b+c, § 33); |*wa/i-ri+i^i* |*ku-ma-na* |*ha-tu-ra+a*, 'because you (are) to write' (ASSUR letters *f*+*g*, § 11).

4.12.2 Conditional Clauses

Conditional conjunctions include *kwati* (REL*(a)-ti*) 'if' and *kwari* (REL+*ra/i*) 'if', the verb stands in the present indicative, often with a future sense. Conditional clauses consist of two parts, protasis (condition, 'if' clause) and apodosis (result). The verb of the apodosis stands in the present indicative or imperative. Conditional clauses appear most frequently in curse formulae: REX-*ta-ti-i-pa-wa/i* REL+*ra/i* REL-*sa-há* ... |*za* |*á-sa-za-ia* ... *wa/i-ta* || *ARHA* |MANUS(-)*i-ti-tu* CAELUM (DEUS)TONITRUS-*hu-za-sá* CAELUM (DEUS)SOL-*za-sá* (DEUS)*i-ia-sá* OMNIS-*MI-zi-ha* DEUS-*ní-zi á-pa* |REX-*hi-sá* |*á-pa-há* "REX"-*na* |*á-pa-há-wa/i* |CAPUT-*ti-na*, 'if anyone from among the kings ... speaks thus ..., may celestial Tarhunzas, the celestial Sun, Eas and all the gods delete that kingdom and that king and that man!" (KARATEPE 1, §§ LIX, LXII, LXXIII, Hu.)

4.12.3 Concessive Clauses

Concessive conjunctions include *kwi* (REL-*i*) 'even though' and *kwa(n)za* (REL-*za*) 'even though', the verb stands in the present or preterite indicative: ^{I}*ka-ma-ni-sa-pa-wa/i* |REL-*i-'* |INFANS-*ní-sa* |*á-sa-tá*, 'even though Kamanis was a child' (KARKAMIŠ A6, § 18); |INFANS-*ni-sa-wa/i-sá* || |REL-*za á-sa-ta,* 'even though he was a child' (KARKAMIŠ A7, § 5).

4.12.4 Consecutive Clauses

The consecutive conjunction is *kwati* (REL-*ti*) 'so that', the verb stands in the present indicative: |REL-*pa-wá/í-ta* |LOCUS-*ta₄-ta-za-'* |*á-pa-ta-za* |("CASTRUM")*ha+ra/i-ní-sà* |*a-ta* |AEDIFICARE+*MI-ha* |*á-TANA-wa/i-sa-wa/i*(URBS) ‖ |REL-*ti* |(BONUS)*wa/i+ra/i-ia-ma-la* |SOLIUM-*MI-i*, 'so I built fortresses in those places so that Adana might dwell peacefully' (KARATEPE 1, §§ XXIII-XXIV, Hu.).

4.12.5 Relative Clauses

Relative clauses may use all forms of the relative pronoun *kwi-/kwa-* (REL) which is frequently placed after the subject. The verb stands in the present or preterite indicative: |("MALUS₂")*há-ní-ia-ta-ia-pa-wa/i-ta* |REL-*ia* |("TERRA" +*LA+LA*⁽″⁾)*wa/i+ra/i-ri+i a-ta* |*á-sa-ta-'* |*wa/i-ta* ("TERRA")*ta-sà-*REL+*ra/i-ri+i ARHA* *501-*ha-há*, 'the evils which were in the land, I removed out of the land' (KARATEPE 1, §§XII-XIII, Ho.).

4.12.6 Temporal Clauses

Temporal conjunctions include *kuman* 'when' and *kwi* (REL-*i*) 'when', the verb stands in the present or preterite indicative: *wa/i-mu-'* |*ku-ma-na* (DEUS)TONITRUS-*sa* ‖ |*á-ma-za* |*tá-ti-ia<-za>* |("LIGNUM")*sà-la-ha-za* |*pi-ia-ta*, 'when Tarhunzas gave me my paternal succession' (KARKAMIŠ A2+3, § 2); *ARHA-pa-wa/i* REL-*i* PES-*wa/i-i-ha-'* *wa/i-mu-'* *za-a-zi* DEUS-*ni-zi* |*ta-ní-mi-zi* CUM-*ní ARHA* PES-*wa/i-ta*, 'when I came forth, all these gods came forth with me' (KARKAMIŠ A1a, §§ 17-18).

5   Texts

This chapter contains twelve sample texts chosen to illustrate the various literary genres of the Iron Age text corpus and to build up a stock of basic vocabulary and an understanding of frequent grammatical constructions; further, to introduce some of the problems encountered when reading hieroglyphic texts, such as varying sign forms, unknown vocabulary and difficult grammar. Damaged and difficult passages, however, have been reduced to a minimum. As the study of hieroglyphic texts involves coping with different styles and sometimes unusual sign forms, it seemed preferable not to use a computerised hieroglyphic font but drawings. They have been fashioned after *CHLI*, Vol. III, and, where available, photos, plaster casts or original objects. The sample texts consist of building inscriptions, dedications, historical narratives, blessings and curse formulae, a funerary inscription and excerpts from letters. While it is not possible to provide a complete overview of the various text groups, it is hoped that the following will provide a good basis for further study. Bronze Age inscriptions are not included because their largely logographic character poses additional difficulties to the beginner. Seals have been excluded because they do not contain text.

It is suggested that the reader study the sample texts in the given order. The texts are linked to one another in context as far as possible and build up from shorter, simpler inscriptions to longer, more complicated texts. As knowledge of signs, vocabulary and grammar builds up, repetitive explanations will not be given but the reader is encouraged to consult the grammar section, sign list and vocabulary. The introduction of each text will provide some background information on provenance, dating, script and literary aspects, as well as a drawing of the respective inscription and references to the *CHLI* editions. The text is broken up into individual clauses as follows: headed by a drawing of the clause and its translation, each clause will be displayed sign by sign with transliteration, accompanying transcription (cursive), translation (bold) and grammatical analysis (normal print). To facilitate easy recognition, the individual signs are represented as they occur in the text, even though given that we read from left to right all signs should be facing left. Starting with text seven, the hieroglyphic drawing will no longer be dissected into single hieroglyphs and the last three texts will show even longer units of connected text. Note that all transliteration follows that of the *CHLI* editions to facilitate easy cross-reference. Where the Procida Acts assign different sign values, this will be duly noted. A dividing line separates the vocabulary, followed by explanatory notes. A superscript question mark indicates that the meaning of a word is only approximate whereas a question mark in brackets indicates it is uncertain.

As far as possible, the pages have been laid out so that all relevant information will be contained on one (double) page. Last but not least, for purposes of review all but the first one-clause inscription will be reproduced in their entirety, providing a drawing with consecutive transliteration and translation. The reader is encouraged to check whether he has understood signs, grammar and vocabulary, as well as to familiarise himself with the compact form in which texts appear in proper editions.

Before you start reading the texts, a few words of caution. Please note that the transliteration of initial-*a*-final as laid out above, 2.3, and adopted throughout is already an interpretation and you may prefer the more neutral option of transliterating final-*a* as a space filler. Note also that transcription of (partly) logographic spellings is not always possible and often debatable. Please view this as an attempt to show the language hidden behind such writing - but question it, too.

5.1   BABYLON 3

Babylon lay very far east of the Neo-Hittite states, yet excavations have brought to light no less than three hieroglyphic inscriptions of the Iron Age. The most likely explanation is that they were taken as booty during western campaigns and moved to Babylon for the royal collection of Nebuchadrezzar. All three objects, a stele (cf. text 10) and two stone bowls, carry dedications to the Storm-God, the head of the Hittite pantheon.

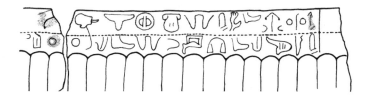

The big stone bowl BABYLON 3 has been restored from several fragments. It has a fluted body and a two-band rim on which a short inscription is incised. Save for a little damage to two signs, the text is complete and tells us that the author, an unknown person called Runtiyas, has donated the bowl to the Storm-God of Aleppo. The writing uses only cursive sign forms which indicates a late date for the object, probably 8th century BC. At this time, Aleppo was still a major cult centre for the Storm-God, and it seems likely that the bowl would have been placed there originally.

📖 *Edition*: Hawkins, 2000, 396–397.

"Runtiyas placed these bowls before the Halabean Tarhunzas"

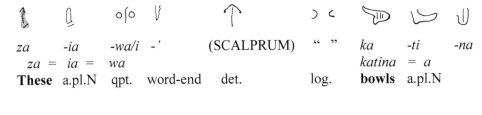

za	-ia	-wa/i	-'	(SCALPRUM)	" "	ka	-ti	-na
za =	ia =	wa				katina	= a	
These	a.pl.N	qpt.	word-end	det.	log.	**bowls**	a.pl.N	

CERVUS$_2$	-ti	-ia	-sa	TONITRUS.	*HALPA*	-pa	-ni
runtiya		= s		*halpa* =	<*wa*>*n* =	*i*	
Runtiyas	n.sg.C			**Halabean**	eth.	d.sg.	

(DEUS)	TONITRUS	-hu	-ti	PRAE	-na	PON[ERE]	-w[a/i]	-ta
Tarhunt		= i		*paran*		*tuwa*	= ta	
Tarhunzas	d.sg.			**before**		**he placed**	3.sg.prt.	

---

za-, 'this'	wan(i)- [ethnic suffix]
-wa [quotative particle]	(DEUS)TONITRUS 'Tarhunzas'
("SCALPRUM")katina-, 'bowls'	[DN]
CERVUS$_2$ 'Runtiyas' [PN]	PRAE = paran, 'before'
TONITRUS.HALPA-pa = 'Halab'	PONERE = tuwa-, 'put, place'
(Aleppo)	

☞ This sentence shows the normal word order object – subject – verb. It is introduced by a particle chain added to the first word of the sentence, here consisting of only one element, the particle -*wa*. Not all particles can or need be translated, i.e. the quotative particle -*wa* is untranslatable. Pronouns, however, should always be translated.

☞ The fourth sign, *450 *a,* appears here without phonetic value, acting as a space filler or word-ender (cf. above, 2.3), transliterated -'.

☞ Logograms often carry phonetic complements giving the ending of the words they represent. If they are followed by a full phonetic spelling, the logogram functions as a determinative and is transliterated in brackets. SCALPRUM, above, is identified as a logogram by the logogram marker ⊃ ⊂, " ", we thus transliterate ("SCALPRUM").

☞ The hieroglyph *HALPA* is transliterated in cursive capitals because it represents a logogram which has been assigned its Luwian reading. Most logograms, meanwhile, are transliterated with Latin words, represented by plain capitals.

☞ The suffix -*wan*- turns *halpa*- 'Halab' into an adjective denominating ethnic origin, 'Halabean'.

☞ Note that preconsonantal *n* as in the name of the Storm-God Tarhunzas is never written, thus (DEUS)TONITRUS-*hu-ti* reads *Tarhunti* (cf. 2.3).

5.2 QAL'AT EL MUDIQ

This inscription, like the following text, comes from the Neo-Hittite state Hama and is named after its find spot Qal'at el Mudiq which is situated north of Hama on the river Orontes. Most Hamathite inscriptions are the work of a King Urahilina (c. 860–840 BC) and of his son Uratamis. The former left amongst other texts three identical building inscriptions of which this is one.

It is a typical example of its genre, consisting of the author's genealogy, narration of building activity, and dedication, in this case to a Semitic goddess, Ba'alat. The writing appears in relief and shows mostly cursive sign forms, although the sheep's head (*110, *ma*) is monumental. Check the sign list for the following signs, they are of somewhat unusual shape: *209 *i,* *210 *ia* and *35 *na*. Note how the orientation of the asymmetrical signs changes with the direction of writing: in the first line, signs face right, indicating a reading direction from right to left, in the second line, as the direction of writing changes, we read from left to right. This alternation is called *boustrophedon*, cf. above, 1.2.1.

📖 *Hamath*: Hawkins 2000: 398–403; *Edition*: Hawkins 2000: 408–409. On the reading Urahilina, s. Yakubovich 2010b: 396 n. 9.

§ 1:

"I (am) Urahilina, son of Paritas, Hamathite King."

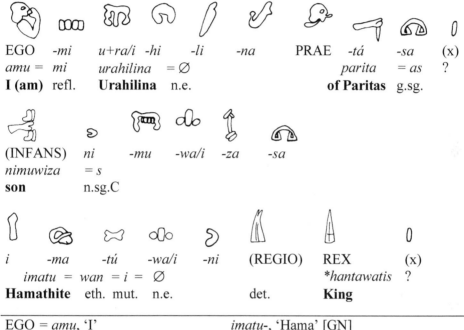

EGO	-mi	u+ra/i	-hi	-li	-na	PRAE	-tá	-sa	(x)
amu =	mi	urahilina		= ∅			parita	= as	?
I (am)	refl.	**Urahilina**		n.e.			**of Paritas**	g.sg.	

(INFANS)	ni	-mu	-wa/i	-za	-sa
nimuwiza	= s				
son	n.sg.C				

i	-ma	-tú	-wa/i	-ni	(REGIO)	REX	(x)
imatu =	wan	= i =	∅			*hantawatis	?
Hamathite	eth.	mut.	n.e.		det.	**King**	

EGO = amu, 'I'

urahilina-, 'Urahilinas' [PN]

PRAE-tà-, 'Paritas' [PN]

INFANS = nimuwiza-, 'son'

imatu-, 'Hama' [GN]

imatu-wan(i)-, 'Hamathite'

REGIO, 'country' [det. of place names]

REX = *hantawat(i)-, 'king'

☞ 𓁹 u+ra consists of two signs in ligature: 𓁹 u + the sign ǀ ra/i which is always attached to another sign. The function of the single vertical (x) after Paritas and REX is unclear - the sentence appears complete without it.

☞ This is a nominal sentence omitting the verb 'to be'. Grammatically, it requires the use of the reflexive pronoun (cf. 4.6.3.). It is not used for emphasis and need not be translated.

☞ Both urahilina- and imatuwan(i)- lack the expected ending of the n.sg.C, ending in -s. Such an omission of case endings is commonly found with logographic writing but one does not expect it with phonetic writing. Note, meanwhile, that the mutation vowel of imatuwan(i)- is written.

§ 2:

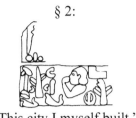

"This city I myself built,"

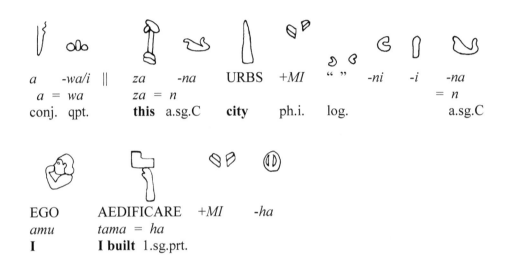

a	-wa/i	‖	za	-na	URBS	+MI	" "	-ni	-i	-na
a	= wa		za	= n						= n
conj.	qpt.		**this** a.sg.C		**city**	ph.i.	log.			a.sg.C

EGO	AEDIFICARE	+MI	-ha
amu	*tama* = *ha*		
I	**I built** 1.sg.prt.		

---

a-, 'and'	EGO = *amu*, 'I'
URBS+*MI*, 'city'	AEDIFICARE+*MI* = *tama*-, 'to build'

☞ The double vertical lines ‖ indicate the end of the line and have no other usage than to aid easy identification of text passages. Note that the continuation of a word from one line to another is not uncommon.

☞ The four parallel strokes of hieroglyph *mi* can be separated into two pairs. When written in ligature with another sign (transliterated +), it functions as a phonetic indicator, possibly representing an *m* in the stem of the word. It is transliterated in cursive capitals and not read phonetically as the syllable *mi*.

☞ The Luwian word for city, here written with the logogram URBS and part of its stem, is unknown.

☞ The writing of EGO before the verb must be understood as emphatic, because the person 'I' is already contained in the verbal ending, therefore 'I myself built'.

§ 3:

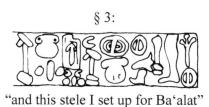

"and this stele I set up for Ba'alat"

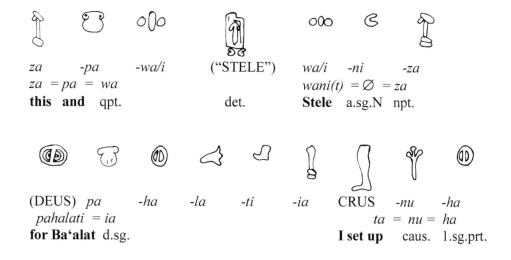

za	-pa	-wa/i	("STELE")	wa/i	-ni	-za
za = pa = wa				wani(t) = Ø = za		
this and qpt.			det.	**Stele** a.sg.N npt.		

(DEUS) pa	-ha	-la	-ti	-ia	CRUS	-nu	-ha
pahalati = ia					ta = nu = ha		
for Ba'alat d.sg.					**I set up** caus. 1.sg.prt.		

-pa, 'but, also'	(DEUS)pahalati-, 'Ba'alat' [DN]
(STELE)wani(t)-, 'stele'	CRUS-nu- = tanu-, 'cause to stand = set up'

☞ Note the logograms markers identifying the determinative STELE. wani(t)- carries a zero ending for the accusative singular plus the neuter particle -sa/-za which is commonly added to neuter words in the nom. and acc. sg. The word final stop -t- is regularly lost, even before the neuter particle.

☞ Ba'alat is a semitic goddess whose name means 'lady, mistress'. Because hieroglyphic, like cuneiform, did not have a letter Ayin ('), h was used as a substitute.

☰ Read the entire text and check whether you have understood it.

1. § 1 EGO-*mi u+ra/i-hi-li-na* PRAE-*tà-sa* (x) (INFANS)*ni-mu-wa/i-za-sa*
    i-ma-tu-wa/i-ni(REGIO) REX (x)
2. § 2 *a-wa/i* || *za-na* "URBS+*MI*"-*ni-i-na* EGO AEDIFICARE+*MI-ha*
    § 3 *za-pa-wa/i* ("STELE")*wa/i-ni-za* (DEUS)*pa-ha-la-ti-ia* CRUS-*nu-ha*

    "I am Urahilina, son of Paritas, Hamathite King.
    This city I built,
    and this stele I set up for Baʻalat."

5.3   HAMA 2

This inscribed building block comes from the Syrian city of Hama (Biblical Hamath) and is one of the very first hieroglyphic inscriptions ever discovered. The earliest report of blocks with strange looking hieroglyphs built into the walls of houses in Hama goes back to 1812. But it was not until 1872 that these blocks were recovered by William Wright, copied and casts taken, and the inscriptions removed to the Museum of İstanbul.

Even though Wright suggested that the strange writing was Hittite, it was initially known as 'Hamathite'. This is hardly surprising if we bear in mind that the discovery antedates the excavations of the Hittite capital and thus virtually all knowledge of the might of the Hittite Empire.

This text, another short building inscription, was written by Urahilina's son Uratamis (c. 840–820 BC). It is one of five very similar inscriptions of his, all of which commemorate the building of fortifications with the help of various river-lands. The style of the writing is very similar to the previous text, and again we encounter some uncommon sign forms, here *35 *na,* *209 *i,* *450 *a* and *176 *la.*

📖 *Discovery*: Sayce, 1903, 60–63; *Edition*: Hawkins, 2000, 411–414.

§ 1:

"I (am) Uratamis, Urahilina's son, Hamathite king."

EGO	-mi	MAGNUS	+ra/i	-tà	-mi	-sa
amu =	mi	uratami	= s			
I (am)	refl.	**Uratamis**	n.sg.C			

u+ra/i	-hi	-li	-na	-sa	(INFANS)	ni	-za	-sa
urahilina	= as				niza =	s		
Urahilina's	g.sg.				**son**	n.sg.C		

i	-ma	-tú	-wa/i	-ni	(REGIO)	REX	‖
imatu	=	wan	= i	= ∅		*hantawatis	
Hamathite	eth.	mut.	n.e.		det.	**king**	

MAGNUS = *ura-*, 'great'
MAGNUS+*ra/i-tà-mi-*, 'Uratamis' [PN]
INFANS = *niza*, short for *nimuwiza-*,'son'

☞ Note the abbreviated form *nizas*, for the word *nimuwizas,* 'son' which appeared in the previous text.

☞ Compare this clause with the opening one of the previous text. They are almost identical but the name of the author of this inscription shows the expected case ending of the nominative singular.

§ 2:

"And I myself built this fortress."

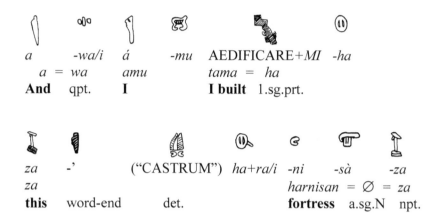

a	-*wa/i*	*á*	-*mu*	AEDIFICARE+*MI*	-*ha*
a = *wa*		*amu*		*tama* = *ha*	
And	qpt.	**I**		**I built**	1.sg.prt.

za	-'	("CASTRUM")	*ha+ra/i*	-*ni*	-*sà*	-*za*
za				*harnisan* = ∅ = *za*		
this	word-end	det.		**fortress**	a.sg.N	npt.

CASTRUM = *harnisa*-, 'fortress'

☞ The inverted word order (verb preceding object) and the use of *amu* 'I' give a certain emphasis to the clause.

☞ Remember that the sign *450 *a* can be used without phonetic value to mark the end of a word, transliterated -'.

☞ *harnisan*, an accusative neuter singular, is followed by the particle *za* which is commonly attached to neuter singulars in the nominative and accusative. Note that the final *n* of the stem, preconsonantal in the current form, is not expressed in writing.

§ 3:

"which the Lakaean river-land made."

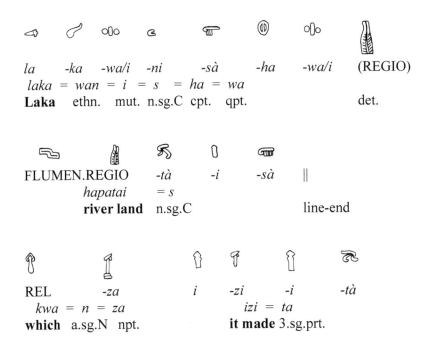

la	*-ka*	*-wa/i*	*-ni*	*-sà*	*-ha*	*-wa/i*	(REGIO)
laka	*= wan*	*= i*	*= s*	*= ha*	*= wa*		
Laka	ethn.	mut.	n.sg.C	cpt.	qpt.		det.

FLUMEN.REGIO	*-tà*	*-i*	*-sà*	‖
	hapatai	*= s*		
	river land	n.sg.C		line-end

REL	*-za*		*i*	*-zi*	*-i*	*-tà*
kwa	*= n*	*= za*		*izi*	*= ta*	
which	a.sg.N	npt.		**it made**	3.sg.prt.	

---

laka-wan(i)-, 'Lakaean' [GN + eth. suff.]   REL = *kwi-/kwa-*, 'who, which'
-ha, 'and' [connective particle]   *izi(ya)-*, 'to make'
FLUMEN.REGIO = *hapata(i)-*, 'river-land'

☞ The relative *kwanza* refers to *harnisanza* of the last clause, and agrees with it in number and gender. Its case is determined by its function in this sentence, here the accusative object. Note that the relative, unlike in English, is not placed sentence initially but, as here, frequently follows the subject.

§ 4:

"And the Land Nikima (is) inside."

a	-tá	-ha	-wa/i	ni	-ki	-ma	-sa	(REGIO)
	anda	= ha	= wa			Nikima	= s	det.
	in(side)	**and**	qpt.			**Nikima**	n.sg.C	**the Land**

---

a-tá = *anda*, 'in(side)'   *nikima-*, 'Nikima' [GN]

☞ The preverb *a-tá* (*anda*) offers another example for the consonant *n* not being written before a consonant.

☞ While determinatives are 'silent' markers of a word, sometimes it may be useful to translate them, especially when referring to names which are not instantly familiar to us, as here 'the land Nikima'.

☞ If you compare this nominal sentence with the one in § 1, you will note that here another form of the verb 'to be' is omitted, namely the 3.sg.prs. It is generally possible to leave out any form of 'to be', not only the indicative but also the imperative (cf. above, 4.1).

⚑   Read the entire text and check whether you have understood it.

HAMA 2

1.   § 1   EGO-*mi* MAGNUS+*ra/i-tà-mi-sa u+ra/i-hi-li-na-sa* (INFANS)*ni-za-
              sa i-ma-tú-wa/i-ni*(REGIO) REX ‖

2.   § 2   *a-wa/i á-mu* AEDIFICARE+*MI-ha za-'* ("CASTRUM")*ha+ra/i-ni-sà-
              za*

      § 3   *la-ka-wa/i-ni-sà-ha-wa/i*(REGIO) FLUMEN.REGIO-*tà-i-sà* ‖ REL-*za*
3.   *i-zi-i-tà*

      § 4   *a-tá-ha-wa/i ni-ki-ma-sa*(REGIO)

      "I (am) Uratamis, Urahilina's son, Hamathite king.
      And I myself built this fortress.
      which the Lakaean river-land made.
      And the Land Nikima (is) therein."

5.4   KARKAMIŠ A1b

The following three texts come from the city of Karkamiš, the single site with the largest number of hieroglyphic inscriptions. Karkamiš was the seat of the Hittite vice-roy during the Bronze age and despite territorial losses the city itself seems to have survived the transition to the Iron Age without major upheaval or destruction.

Controlling an important crossing of the river Euphrates, it continued to be a powerful city state for several more centuries. In 717 it was annexed by Assyria, and destroyed by Nebuchadrezzar in 605. British excavations between 1911–14, resuming in 1920 concentrated on the Lower City; unfortunately, they had to be abandoned due to military conflicts in 1920, and with the Syro-Turkish border now running through the site further excavations are no longer possible. Nonetheless, many hieroglyphic inscriptions and neo-Hittite sculptures were found, dating to the 11–9th centuries BC.

The orthostat KARKAMIŠ A1b belonged to the Long Wall of Sculpture and shows on the right a nude, winged goddess, in the centre a seated female figure, presumably the authoress of the inscription. The woman is depicted holding a spindle and facing right, she raises her left arm in the pose of the hieroglyph EGO, "I". The text shows in the background, to either side of her head. Carved in relief, it uses only monumental sign forms which albeit damaged in parts are fairly legible. The text is a dedication of BONUS-tis, the wife of the ruler Suhis (II), who built the Long Wall of sculpture and presumably erected this monument for his wife after her death. The text is therefore dateable to the 10th century BC.

📖   *Edition*: Hawkins, 2000, 91–92.

§ 1:

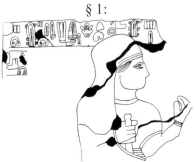

"I (am) BONUS-tis, the dear wife of the Country-
Lord Suhis."

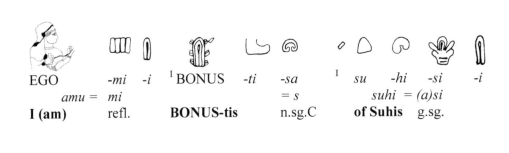

EGO	-mi	-i	ᴵ BONUS	-ti	-sa	ᴵ su	-hi	-si	-i
amu =	mi				= s	suhi =	(a)si		
I (am)	refl.		**BONUS-tis**		n.sg.C	**of Suhis**	g.sg.		

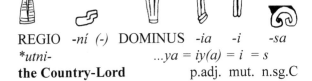

REGIO	-ní (-)	DOMINUS	-ia	-i	-sa
*utni-			...ya = iy(a) =	i	= s
the Country-Lord			p.adj.	mut.	n.sg.C

| BONUS	-[m]i	-sa	|| FEMINA	-ti	-i	-sa
	= m(a) = i	= s		wanat =	i =	s
dear	part.	mut. n.sg.C	**woman**	mut.	n.sg.C	

BONUS-*tis* [PN]   BONUS-*ma/i*-, 'dear'
Suhis [PN]   FEMINA = *wanat(i)*-, 'woman'
REGIO-*ni*(-)DOMINUS-*yaiya*-, MATER = *anat(i)*-, 'mother'
   'of the Country-Lord'

☞ As this sentence illustrates, the personal marker ⊘, transliterated ^I, is used to identify both men and women.

☞ Notice how the first and third word, both ending in -*i* are written -*Ci-i*. The function of this plene writing is not clear.

☞ The phonetic reading of the name BONUS-*tis* is not known because the logogram BONUS is used for several words of different stems.

☞ The beginning of a new word can be indicated with the marker ₢, transliterated |. While helpful to us, this graphic practice was unfortunately neither binding nor necessarily consistent within any single text.

☞ REGIO-*ni*(-)DOMINUS, "Country-Lord" is known on seals originally as the title of a provincial governor. The city of Karkamiš seems to have had two competing dynastic lines, with the respective titles of "Great King" or "Country-Lord". Although it stands in apposition to the personal name Suhis, it is a possessive adjective in formal agreement with BONUS-*tis*.

☞ The sign *79 is used to write both woman (transliterated FEMINA, Luw. **wanat(i)-*) and mother (MATER, Luw. **anat(i)-*). Thus the transliteration of the sign is already an interpretation.

§ 2:

"Wheresoever my husband honours his own name,"

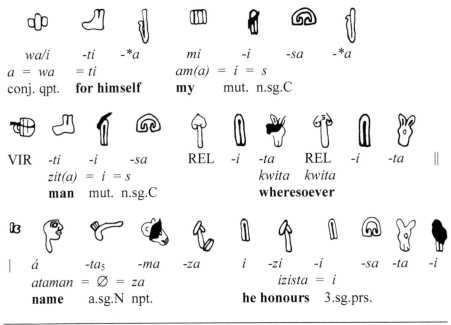

wa/i	-ti	-*a	mi	-i	-sa	-*a
a = wa	= ti		am(a)	= i	= s	
conj. qpt.	**for himself**		**my**	mut.	n.sg.C	

VIR	-ti	-i	-sa	REL	-i	-ta	REL	-i	-ta	‖
	zit(a)	= i	= s		kwita	kwita				
man		mut.	n.sg.C		**wheresoever**					

│ á	-ta₅	-ma	-za	i	-zi	-i	-sa	-ta	-i
ataman	= ∅	= za			izista	= i			
name	a.sg.N	npt.			**he honours**	3.sg.prs.			

-ti, 'for himself/herself'	kwita kwita, 'wheresoever'
ama/i-, 'my'	ataman-, 'name'
VIR = zita/i-, 'man'	izista-, 'to honour'
REL-i-ta = kwita, 'where'	

☞ Note how the first two words are subject to the graphic practice of placing word-initial *a* finally, cf. 2.3. *wa/i-ti-*a* and *mi-i-sa-*a* thus stand for /a=wa=ti/ and /ami=s/ respectively.

☞ The enclitic reflexive pronoun *-ti*, 'for himself' can be translated together with the object *atamanza* as 'his own name' (lit. 'the name for himself'); cf. 4.2.3.

☞ Reduplicated *kwita* (REL-*i-ta*), 'where', becomes indefinite, 'wheresoever'.

☞ For *ataman-* cf. also Rieken–Yakubovich 2010: 203.

§ 3:

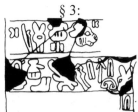

"he shall also honour me with goodness"

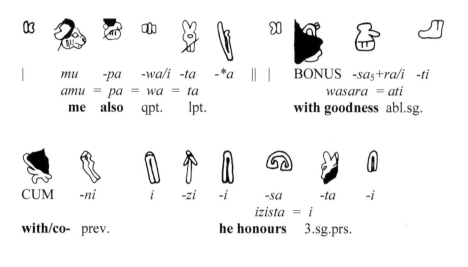

	mu	-pa	-wa/i	-ta	-*a	‖		BONUS	-sa₅+ra/i	-ti
	amu	= pa	= wa	= ta					wasara	= ati
	me	**also**	qpt.	lpt.				**with goodness**	abl.sg.

CUM	-ní		i	-zi	-i		-sa	-ta	-i
							izista	= i	
with/co-	prev.						**he honours**	3.sg.prs.	

-*mu*, '(for) me'   BONUS = *wasar(a)-*, 'goodness'
-*ata*, 'he, she, it; they'

☞ The ablative *wasarati* 'with goodness' has instrumental force.

Read the entire text and check whether you have understood it.

1.   § 1 EGO-*mi-i* [I]BONUS-*ti-sa* [I]*su-hi-si-i* REGIO-*ní*(-)DOMINUS-*ia-i-sa*
2. |BONUS-*mi-sa* ‖ FEMINA-*ti-i-sa*
     § 2 *wa/i-ti-*a mi-i-sa-*a* VIR-*ti-i-sa* REL-*i-ta* REL-*i-ta* ‖ |*á-ta₅-ma-za i-zi-*
3.   *i-sa-ta-i*
     § 3 |*mu-pa-wa/i-ta-*a* ‖ |BONUS-*sa₅+ra/i-ti* CUM-*ní i-zi-i-sa-ta-i*

    "I (am) BONUS-tis, the dear wife of the Country-Lord Suhis.
    Wheresoever my husband honours his own name,
    he shall also honour me with goodness."

5.5   KARKAMIŠ A4d

This one-line inscription belonged to the statue of a god seated on his throne, identified by the inscription as Atrisuhas ('soul-of-Suhis'). The throne once rested on a pair of lions held by a bird-headed figure between them. The god himself had an axe in his left and a mace in his right hand and wore a long robe. The inscription was placed the bottom of it like a decorative border.

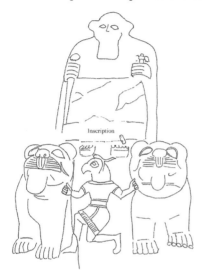

The monument was discovered during the Karkamiš excavation of 1911-14, broken into many fragments. It was restored, the text alone reconstructed from 17 fragments. Unfortunately, shortly after the text and monument were pieced together, they were again destroyed and are now lost.

Despite the damage to the inscription, the text is easily restorable. In the following, the text is displayed as preserved but where hieroglyphs are shown individually, drawings of the lost signs (with dotted lines) are also given. Naturally, this can only be a suggestion of how the lost signs may have looked.

The text consists of a short curse, an epigraph to the neighbouring portal orthostat KARKAMIŠ A11a, a building inscription of Katuwas, king of Karkamiš in the 10th or early 9th century BC.

📖 *Edition*: Hawkins, 2000, 100–101.

§ 1:

"For this god Atrisuhas with the gods, (he) who does
not [give] annual bread, an ox and two sheep"

za	[-ti]	-pa	-wa/i	(DEUS)	á	-tara/i	-su	-ha
zat	= i	= pa	= wa		atrisuha	= a		
for this	d.sg.	cpt.	qpt.		**Atrisuhas**	d.sg.		

DEUS	-ni	-za	⌈CUM⌉	-ni	ANNUS	-sa	-li	-z[a]	-n[a]
masani	= anza				usaliza	= n			
the gods	d.pl.		**with**		**annual**	a.sg.C			

(PANIS)	tú+ra/i	-p[i]	-n[a]	BOS (ANIMAL)	2	OVIS (ANIMAL)
turp(a)	= i	= n		waw(a) = i = n	tuwinzi	haw(a) = i = nzi
bread	mut.	a.sg.C		**ox** mut. a.sg.C	**two**	**sheep** mut. a.pl.C

REL	-[sa]	NEG[2]		[DARE]	-i
kwi	= s	na		piya	= i
(he) who	n.sg.C	**not**		**he gives**	3.sg. prs.

Atrisuha-, 'Atrisuhas' [PN]	BOS = *wawa/i-*, 'ox'
DEUS = *masana/i-*, 'god'	OVIS = *hawa/i-*, 'sheep'
ANNUS = *usaliza-*, 'annual'	NEG₂ = *na(wa)*, 'not'
PANIS = *turpa/i-*, 'bread'	DARE = *piya-*, 'to give'

☞ The curse is divided into two parts, the first, this clause, states the condition and is called protasis. Its verb always stands in the present indicative.

☞ The name of the god Atrisuhas can be analysed as *atri* 'soul, image' + *suhas* 'of Suhis'. Only this inscription, and the related KARKAMIŠ A11a, which mentions the building of this monument, attest this deity. Presumably, it refers to the deified Suhis, ancestor of the author Katuwas.

☞ The d.pl. *masaninza* shows an unexplained stem *masani-*, possibly with contraction /-iya-/ > /i/. This form occurs in a few other texts as well (e.g. see below, KARKAMIŠ A11b+c § 18a) while the expected stem *masana-* is well attested in the dative plural.

☞ *zati* could be one of two forms which look identical: 1. as above, the dat.sg. which adds -*i* to the suffixed stem of the dative, *zat-*; 2. the adverb *zati*, 'here'. Not only *za-* but also the demonstrative *apa-* and the relative *kwi/a-* use a dental stems extension in the dative; cf. above, 3.2.5.

§2:

"may Atrisuhas come fatally against him!"

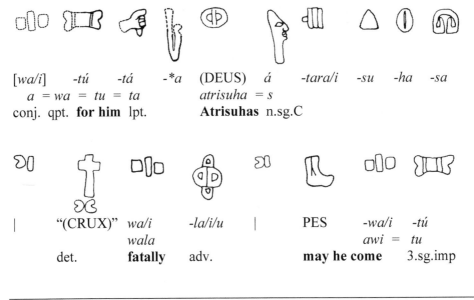

[wa/i]	-tú	-tá	-*a	(DEUS) á	-tara/i	-su	-ha	-sa
a = wa	= tu	= ta		atrisuha = s				
conj. qpt.		**for him**	lpt.	**Atrisuhas** n.sg.C				

	"(CRUX)"	wa/i	-la/i/u		PES	-wa/i	-tú
		wala				awi =	tu
det.		**fatally**	adv.		**may he come**		3.sg.imp

-tu, '(for) him'   wala [adv., det. CRUX], 'ill, fatally'
-ta [locative particle]   PES = awi-, 'to come'

☞ The second part of the curse is called apodosis and names the resulting consequences of the previously stated condition. Its verb always stands in the present imperative.

☞ Do not worry if signs such as here la/i/u (*445) differ from the version given in the sign list, as long as the general shape of the sign is still recognisable. A certain amount of variation must be expected, just as our handwriting varies from person to person.

🕮 Read the entire text and check whether you have understood it.

§ 1 *za*[-*ti*]-*pa-wa/i* (DEUS)*á-tara/i-su-ha* DEUS-*ni-za* ⌈CUM⌉-*ni* ANNUS-*sa-li-z*[*a*] -*n*[*a*] (PANIS)*tú+ra/i-p*[*i*]-*n*[*a*] BOS(ANIMAL) 2 OVIS (ANIMAL) REL-[*sa*] NEG₍₂₎ |[DARE]-*i*

§ 2 [*wa/i*]-*tú-tá-*a* (DEUS) *á-tara/i-su-ha-sa* |"(CRUX)"*wa/i-la/i/u* |PES-*wa/i-tú*

"For this god Atrisuhas with the gods,
(he) who does not [give] annual bread, an ox and two sheep:
may Atrisuhas come fatally against him!"

5.6   KARKAMIŠ A4b

This stele bears an inscription commemorating a victory of Ura-Tarhunzas, king of Karkamiš, who presumably reigned in the 11th or 10th century BC. The stele was set up at a later date by the son of the ruler Suhis, who was a priest of the goddess Kubabas.

The incised inscription uses only monumental sign forms and shows a deliberately archaising style. This is achieved by various means. For instance, words are more often written logographically than phonetically - this has a serious disadvantage for us because it means that grammatical endings are not recorded. Endings are even occasionally omitted with phonetic spellings. The genealogy, especially the titles MAGNUS.REX 'Great King' and HEROS 'Hero', recalls seal legends and cuneiform texts from the time of the Hittite Empire. Further, the determinative of the city of Karkamiš changed from Bronze to Iron Age. Because the city had lost its previous power over outside territories, it no longer took the determinative REGIO 'land' but URBS 'city'.

Nonetheless, one can also detect features typical for Iron Age inscriptions, which betray the true age of this text. Here we must name the recording of particle chains, also the frequent omission of the sentence-initial conjunction *a-*, as well as the use of sign forms specific to the Iron Age.

📖   *Edition*: Hawkins (2000), 80–82.

§1:

"Great King, Ura-Tarhunzas, Great King, Hero,
king of the land of Karkamiš, son of X-pa-zitis, Great King, Hero".

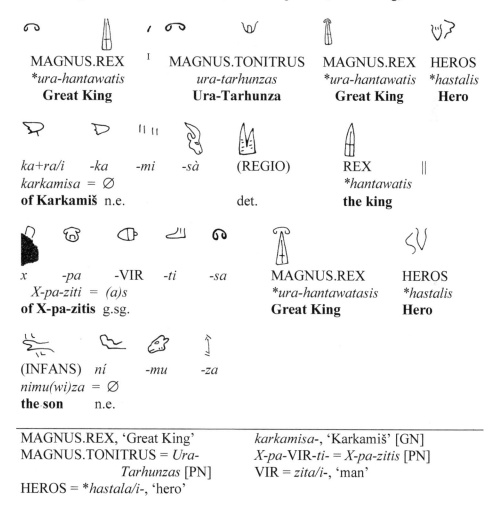

MAGNUS.REX	ᴵ	MAGNUS.TONITRUS	MAGNUS.REX	HEROS
*ura-hantawatis		ura-tarhunzas	*ura-hantawatis	*hastalis
Great King		**Ura-Tarhunza**	**Great King**	**Hero**

ka+ra/i	-ka	-mi	-sà	(REGIO)	REX	‖
karkamisa = ∅					*hantawatis	
of Karkamiš n.e.				det.	**the king**	

x	-pa	-VIR	-ti	-sa	MAGNUS.REX	HEROS
X-pa-ziti = (a)s					*ura-hantawatasis	*hastalis
of X-pa-zitis g.sg.					**Great King**	**Hero**

(INFANS)	ní	-mu	-za
nimu(wi)za = ∅			
the son	n.e.		

MAGNUS.REX, 'Great King'	karkamisa-, 'Karkamiš' [GN]
MAGNUS.TONITRUS = Ura-	X-pa-VIR-ti- = X-pa-zitis [PN]
Tarhunzas [PN]	VIR = zita/i-, 'man'
HEROS = *hastala/i-, 'hero'	

☞ VIR, the Iron Age variant (*313) rather than the Empire form (*312) betrays
the inscription's age.

§ 2:

"Against him came(?) forth a quarrel from the land Sura(?),"

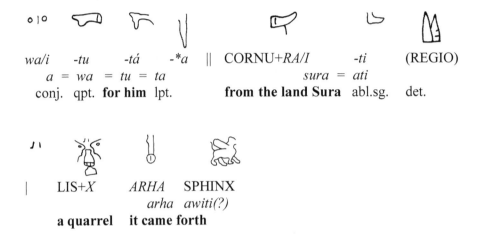

wa/i	-tu	-tá	-*a	‖	CORNU+*RA/I*		-ti	(REGIO)
a =	*wa* =	*tu* =	*ta*		*sura* =		*ati*	
conj.	qpt.	**for him**	lpt.		**from the land Sura**		abl.sg.	det.

	LIS+*X*	*ARHA*	SPHINX
		arha	*awiti(?)*
	a quarrel	**it came forth**	

CORNU+*RA/I* = *sura-*, [GN]   *arha*, 'forth, away'
LIS, 'quarrel, lawsuit'   SPHINX = *awiti-*(?), 'sphinx'

☞ *wa/i-tu-tá-*a* is a modern element in this inscription; introductory particle chains are not a common feature of the Bronze Age.

☞ On the place name Sura, s. most recently Simon 2009.

☞ The sign *24 LIS consists of two faces looking at each other above a seal, cf. below, § 5. Here, an extra element appears below the seal, possibly the outline of the sign *sa* or *sa₅*, maybe indicating the nominative ending -*s*.

☞ SPHINX, following the preverb *arha*, seems to represent the verb. Captivating is Singer's interpretation[34] that the present writing is a play on sound: the word for 'sphinx' was *awiti-*, identical with the 3.sg.prs. of *awi-*, 'to come'; used here, if interpreted correctly, as a historical present; cf. 4.7.2.

34 quoted in Hawkins, 2000, 81.

§ 3:

"and one put the army against."

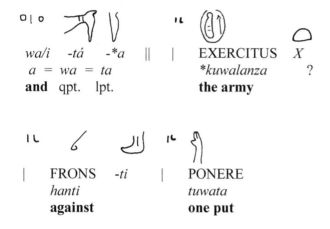

wa/i	-tá	-*a	‖	EXERCITUS	X
a =	wa =	ta		*kuwalanza	?
and	qpt.	lpt.		**the army**	

	FRONS	-ti		PONERE
	hanti			tuwata
	against			**one put**

EXERCITUS = *kuwalan-, 'army'   FRONS-ti = hanti, 'against'

☞ An object to *hanti* (FRONS-*ti*) 'against' seems to be missing.

☞ The meaning of the sign behind EXERCITUS is not clear. Could it be a logogram providing the desired object to *hanti*, or is it an addition to EXERCITUS?

§ 4:

"The mighty Storm-god (and) Kubabas gave
a mighty courage (to) the king Ura-Tarhunzas,"

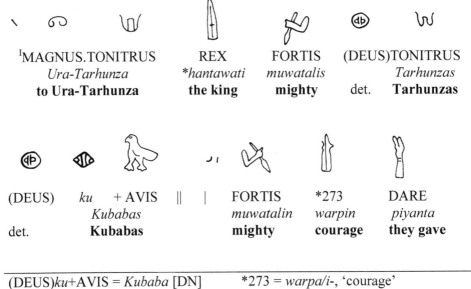

[I]MAGNUS.TONITRUS	REX	FORTIS	(DEUS)TONITRUS
Ura-Tarhunza	**hantawati*	*muwatalis*	*Tarhunzas*
to Ura-Tarhunza	**the king**	**mighty**	det. **Tarhunzas**

(DEUS)	*ku* + AVIS	‖ |	FORTIS	*273	DARE
	Kubabas		*muwatalin*	*warpin*	*piyanta*
det.	**Kubabas**		**mighty**	**courage**	**they gave**

(DEUS)*ku*+AVIS = *Kubaba* [DN]   *273 = *warpa/i-*, 'courage'
FORTIS = *muwatala/i-*, 'mighty'

☞ Asyndetic coupling of a pair, here Tarhunzas and Kubabas, is not uncommon
   in Luwian.
☞ Kubabas, chief goddess of Karkamiš, incorporates her hieroglyphic symbol
   'bird' as a logogram somewhat unusually after the first syllable of her name.
☞ Note that this clause does not contain a single full phonetic writing.

§ 5:

"and by (his) mighty [courage] he resolved the quarrel."

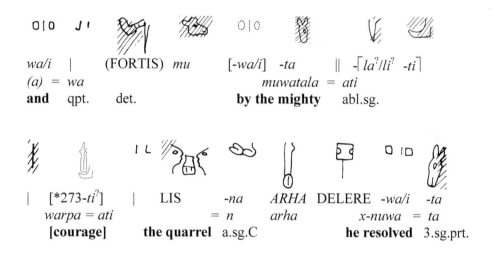

wa/i		(FORTIS) mu		[-wa/i] -ta	‖ -⌈la²/li² -ti⌉
(a) = wa		det.		muwatala = ati	
and	qpt.			**by the mighty**	abl.sg.

	[*273-ti²]		LIS	-na	ARHA	DELERE	-wa/i	-ta
	warpa = ati			= n	arha		x-nuwa	= ta
	[courage]		the quarrel	a.sg.C			he resolved	3.sg.prt.

ARHA DELERE, 'to destroy completely; resolve'

☞ As happens frequently in later periods, here the initial *a* of *awa* seems to have been omitted altogether. This is uncharacteristic for this inscription, compare the particle chains of §§ 2, 3 and 6.

☞ The reconstructed ablative *273-*ti* is used as an instrumental (*wherewith*? - 'by his mighty courage').

§ 6:

"Arnu-x, son of the ruler Suhis, priest of Kubaba, erected this stele."

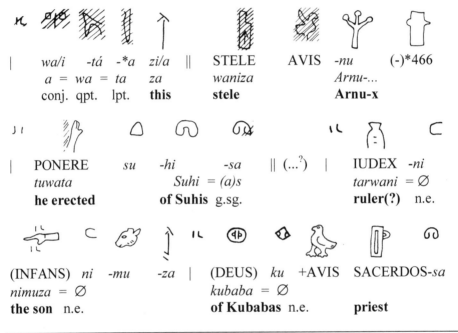

	wa/i	-tá	-*a	zi/a	‖	STELE	AVIS	-nu	(-)*466
	a =	wa =	ta	za		waniza		Arnu-...	
	conj.	qpt.	lpt.	**this**		**stele**		**Arnu-x**	

	PONERE	su	-hi	-sa	‖ (...?)		IUDEX	-ni
	tuwata		Suhi = (a)s				tarwani = ∅	
	he erected		**of Suhis** g.sg.				**ruler(?)** n.e.	

(INFANS)	ni	-mu	-za		(DEUS)	ku	+AVIS	SACERDOS-sa
nimuza = ∅					kubaba = ∅			
the son n.e.					**of Kubabas** n.e.			**priest**

STELE = tanisa-, wanit-, 'stele'   IUDEX = tarwani-, 'ruler(?)'
AVIS-nu(-)*466, Arnu-(wantis?) [PN]   SACERDOS 'priest'

☞ The sign representing the pronoun za is used as an archaising feature. In the Bronze Age it read zi/a but when this text was written, the two differentiated signs zi (*376) and za (*377) were already in use, compare the za of nimuza.

☞ The logogram STELE is known to represent two different words, tanisa- and wani(t)-, both meaning 'stele'. The above transcription waniza (the word final stop would be deleted, cf. 2.4) is therefore only a suggestion.

☞ The meaning of the logogram *466 is unknown. A common name beginning in Arnu- would be Arnuwantis but we simply do not know what to read here.

☞ For the meaning of tarwani-, s. Giusfredi 2009.

☵ Read the entire text and check whether you have understood it.

1. § 1   MAGNUS.REX ᴵMAGNUS.TONITRUS
         MAGNUS.REX
2.   HEROS *ka+ra/i-ka-mi-sà*(REGIO) REX ||
         x-pa-VIR-*ti-sa* MAGNUS.REX HEROS
         (INFANS)*ní-mu-za*
3. § 2   *wa/i-tu-tá-*a* || CORNU+RA/I-ti*(REGIO)
         |LIS *ARHA* SPHINX
4. § 3   *wa/i-tá-*a* || |EXERCITUS-*X* |FRONS-*ti*
         |PONERE
   § 4   ᴵMAGNUS.TONITRUS REX FORTIS
         (DEUS)TONITRUS
5.   (DEUS)*ku+*AVIS || |FORTIS *273 DARE
6. § 5   *wa/i* |(FORTIS)*mu-[wa/i]-ta*||-⌈ *la?/li?-ti*⌉
         |[*273-*ti?*] |LIS-*na ARHA* DELERE-*wa/i-*
         ta
7. § 6 |*wa/i-tá-*a zi/a* || STELE AVIS-*nu*(-)*466
         |PONERE *su-hi-sa* ||(...?)
8. |IUDEX-*ni* |(INFANS)*ni-mu-za* |(DEUS)
         *ku+*AVIS SACERDOS-*sa*

"Great King, Ura-Tarhunzas, Great King, Hero, king of the land of Karkamiš,
son of X-pa-zitis, Great King, Hero.
Against him came(?) forth a quarrel from the land Sura(?),
and one put the army against.
The mighty Storm-god (and) Kubabas gave a mighty courage (to) the king Ura-
Tarhunzas,
and by (his) mighty [courage] he resolved the quarrel.
Arnu-x, son of the ruler Suhis, priest of Kubabas, erected this stele."

5.7 MARAŞ 1

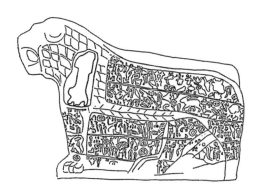

Hieroglyphic stone inscriptions have been found as reliefs on natural rock surfaces, as well as on stelae, building blocks and some sculptured elements, notably portal lions. One such lion was discovered in the late nineteenth century AD at the citadel gate of the city of Maraş, once the capital of the neo-Hittite state Gurgum. It bears a commemorative inscription of Halparuntiyas III who can be dated to the 9th century BC.

In the following, we shall look at the beginning of the text which includes some common topoi of royal inscriptions. As expected, it begins with the author's genealogy which is remarkably extensive and introduces many words expressing family relationship. In the following clauses, Halparuntiyas claims to have received preferred treatment by the gods. Similar statements can be found in many inscriptions. They serve both to support the author's claim to greatness and to justify his deeds as willed by the gods. The text continues with this theme along the lion's body, thereafter possibly on another, now lost element. The relief writing changes between monumental and cursive sign forms although a few signs appear only in their cursive variant.

Starting with this text, the passages under discussion while still heading each page will no longer be presented sign by sign. The more common signs should now be familiar to you, and all signs can be checked in the sign list. While there will also be new signs, they will not be commented on if regular and unproblematic. Note that if two clauses are discussed on one page, the headers will show both drawings as they appear on the lion; the paragraph numbers and, of course, the direction of writing will tell you which is to be read first.

📖 *Edition:* Hawkins, 2000, 261–265.

§ 1a:

"I (am) Halparuntiyas, the ruler, Gurgumean king."

EGO-*wa/i-mi-i* ^ITONITRUS.*HALPA-pa-ru-ti-i-ia-sa*
amu = *wa* = *mi*   *Halpa* = *runtiya* = *s*
I (am) qpt. **myself** **Halparuntiyas** n.sg.C

|"(IUDEX)"*tara/i-wa/i-ni-sà* |*ku+ra/i-ku-ma-wa/i-ni-i-sà*(URBS)
 tarwani = *s*   *kurkuma* = *wan* = *i* = *s*
the ruler(?) n.sg.C **Gurgumean** eth. mut. n.sg.C

REX-*ti-i-sa*
*hantawat = *i* = *s*
king   mut. n.sg.C

-mi, 'myself'
^ITONITRUS.*HALPA-paruntiya-*, 'Halparuntiyas' [PN]
kurkuma(URBS), 'Gurgum' (Maraş) [GN]

☞ The text begins on the left shoulder of the lion with a badly preserved large figure pointing at itself, the sign EGO. It is peculiar that the ruler figure is standing on a lion, a pose normally associated with the depiction of gods. Hawkins suggests it may indicate that this is an inscription of a posthumously deified ruler.[35]

☞ On the use of personal plus reflexive pronoun, cf. 4.6.

☞ The sign order sometimes takes aesthetic considerations into account, see how the sign *pa* is used to fill the space left between the sign *HALPA* and *i*.

35 Hawkins, 2000, 262.

§ 1b:

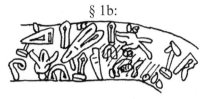

"the son of Laramas the governor"

¹*la+ra/i+a-ma-si-i-sa* |LEPUS+*ra/i-ia-li-i-sa*
  Larama = *as(a)* = *i* = *s*   **tapariyal(a)* = *iy(a)* = *i* = *s*
of Laramas p.adj. mut. n.sg.C   **gubernatorial** p.adj. mut. n.sg.C

|INFANS-*mu-wa/i-za-sá*
nimuwiza = *s*
son   n.sg.C

---

¹*larama*-, 'Laramas' [PN]   LEPUS+*rayala/i*- = **tapariyala/i*-,
                                        'governor'

☞   *la+ra/i+a* (*178): The two double strokes represent a cursive form of
    hieroglyph *450 *a*, which can also be seen differentiating the sign pairs *i* and
    ia, *zi* and *za*.
☞ The syntax of this clause may seem complicated: the personal name Laramas
    forms a possessive adjective in -*asi*-, modifying *nimuwizas*, lit. 'the
    Laramian son', i.e. 'the son of Laramas'. Like all adjectives, it takes its case
    ending, number and gender in agreement with the noun it qualifies. Larama's
    title follows his name in the shape of a derived possessive adjective, this
    time in -*iya*-, again agreeing with *nimuwizas*. We cannot and should not
    imitate this contruction in English.

§ 1c:

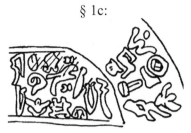

"grandson of the hero Halparuntiyas"

ᴵTONITRUS.*HALPA-pa-ru-ti-ia-si-sà*   HEROS-*li-sa*
    Halparunti = as(a) = i   = s   **hastali(ya) = i = s*
of Halparuntiyas   p.adj. mut. n.sg.C   **of the hero**   mut. n.sg.C

|(INFANS.NEPOS)*ha-ma-si-sá-'*
    hams(a) = i = s
grandson   mut. n.sg.C

(INFANS.NEPOS)*hamsa/i-,*
'grandson'

☞ The use of the final hieroglyph, *450 *a*, in the word *hamsis* is another good example of it being used to mark the end of the word, transliterated with an apostrophe. A phonetic value would be inconceivable, as even the vowel of the previous sign is superfluous, the word *hamsi-* ending in the *-s* of the nominative singular.

☞ This clause illustrates one typical difficulty: to analyse the form HEROS-*li-sa*, we must choose on limited evidence whether it is a true *i*-stem **hastali-* or an *a*-stem with *i*-mutation **hastala/i-*. The choice here is only tentative but affects our analysis of the form: if dealing with a true *i*-stem, we would have a gen.sg. in *–(a)s*, if dealing with an *a*-stem, we would have a possessive adjective in *–iy(a)* with *i*-mutation and the ending of the n.sg.C. The same problem occurs in the following clauses with the words *warpalis* and *tarwanis*.

§ 1e: § 1d:

"great-great-grandson of the   "great-grandson of the brave Muwatalis"
   ruler Halparuntiyas"

§ 1d   *mu-wa/i-ta-li-si-sà* |("SCALPRUM+*RA/I.LA/I/U*")*wa/i+ra/i-pa-li-sa*
       Muwatali = (a)s(a) = i = s   *warpali(ya) = i = s*
   of Muwatalis p.adj. mut. n.sg.C   **of the brave**   mut. n.sg.C

|(INFANS.NEPOS)*ha-ma-su-ka-la-sá*
   hamsukala = s
great-grandson   n.sg.C

§ 1e   [I]*TONITRUS.HALPA-pa*-CERVUS₂-*ti-ia-si-sà*
        Halparunti = as(a) = i = s
       of Halparuntiyas   p.adj.   mut. n.sg.C

|("IUDEX")*tara/i-wa/i-ni-sá* |(INFANS)*na-wa/i-sa*
tarwani = (a)s   *nawa = s*
ruler(?)   g.sg.   **great-great-grandson**   n.sg.C

---

muwatali-, 'Muwatalis' [PN]
(SCALPRUM+*RA/I.LA/I/U*)*warpala/i-*, 'brave'
(INFANS.NEPOS)*hamsukala-*, 'great-grandson'
[I]TONITRUS.HALPA-*pa*-CERVUS₂-*tiya-*, 'Halparuntiyas' [PN]
(INFANS)*nawa-*, 'great-great-grandson'

☞ The logogram SCALPRUM above takes two phonetic indicators, *RA/I* and
   LA/I/U, representing respectively the *r* and *li* of *warpali*.

§ 1f: § 1g:

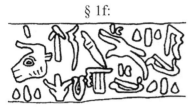   

"great-great-great-grandson of the hero   "descendant of the governor Laramas"
Muwizis"

§ 1f ¹*mu-wa/i-zi-si*   HEROS-*li-sà* |(INFANS)*na-wa/i-na-wa/i-sá*
  Muwizi = *(a)si*   **hastali(ya)* =*i* = *s*   *nawanawa* = *s*
of Muwizis   g.sg. **of the hero** mut. n.sg.C **gr.-gr.-great-grandson** n.sg.C

§ 1g ¹*la+ra/i+a-ma-si-sá*   LEPUS+*ra/i-ia-li-sa*
  Larama = *as(a)* = *i* = *s*   **tapariyal(a)* = *iy(a)* = *i* = *s*
of Laramas p.adj. mut. g.sg.   **gubernatorial** p.adj. mut. n.sg.C

|(INFANS)*ha+ra/i-tu-sá*
  hartu = *s*
descendant n.sg.C

---

¹*muwizi*-, 'Muwizis' [PN]
(INFANS)*nawanawa*-, 'great-great-great-grandson'
(INFANS)*hartu*-, 'descendant'

☞Compare the shape of the *la* in Laramas with the simpler version
encountered in § 1b.

§ 1h:

"(I am) the king loved by the gods, known by the people, heard of abroad,"

DEUS-*na-ti*	(LITUUS)*á-za-mi-sà*	CAPUT-*ta-ti*
masana = ati	aza = am(a) = i = s	= ati
by the gods abl.	**loved** part. mut. n.sg.C	**by the people** abl.

⌈(LITUUS)⌉*u-ni-mi-sá*	|FINES-*ha-ti*
uni = (a)m(a) = i = s	irha = ati
known part. mut. n.sg.C	**by the borders** abl. = **abroad**

AUDIRE-*mi-sà*	REX-*ti-sá*
*tuma(n)ti = (a)m(a) = i = s	*hantawat = i = s
heard of part. mut. n.sg.C	**king** mut. n.sg.C

DEUS = *masana/i-*, 'god'	(LITUUS)*uni-*, 'to know'
(LITUUS)*aza-*, 'to love'	FINES = *irha/i-*, 'border'
CAPUT, 'man'	AUDIRE =**tuma(n)ti-*, 'to hear'

☞ One of the functions of the ablative, as this clause illustrates, is to express the agent of a passive participle. Note that to date no passive indicative forms of the past are attested which may suggest that past passive activities were always expressed with the participle.

§ 1i:

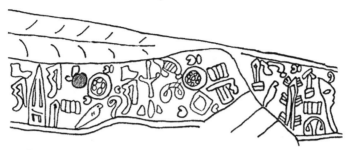

"the loved, exalted, satisfying(?), honey-sweet king,"

(LITUUS)*á-za-mi-sa* |(BONUS)*u-li-ia-mi-sà*
  aza = *am(a)* = *i* = *s*   *uliya* = *am(a)* = *i* = *s*
loved   part.   mut. n.sg.C   **exalted**   part.   mut. n.sg.C

|("PANIS.SCUTELLA")*mu-sa*ʾ*-nu-wa/i-ti-sá* |("PANIS")*ma-li-⌈ri+i⌉-mi-i-sá*
  musanuwa = *ant* = *i* = *s*   *maliri* = *(a)m(a)* = *i* = *s*
satisfying(?) part. mut. n.sg.C   **honey-sweet** part. mut. n.sg.C

REX-*ti-sá*
*hantawat = *i* = *s*
king   mut. n.sg.C

(BONUS)*uliya-/waliya-*, 'to exalt'
musanu-, 'cause to satisfy, satiate'
("PANIS.SCUTELLA")*musanuwant(i)-*, 'satisfying(?)'
("PANIS")*malitima/i-*, 'honey-sweet'

☞ *mu-sa*ʾ*-nu-wa/i-ti-sá*: the sign *sa*ʾ closely resembles the sign *hi*.
☞ Note the difference between the active participal in -*ant(i)*- and the passive participle in -*mi*-.
☞ *malirimi-* seems to be connected with *malit-*, 'honey', and may be derived from a denominal verb meaning 'to sweeten, make pleasant'. It shows rhotacism from /d/ > /r/.

§ 2:

"and my paternal gods loved me,"

|wa/i-mu	|á-mi-i-zi	|tá-ti-zi	DEUS-ni-zi-i
(a) = wa = mu	am(a) = i = nzi	tatiy(a) = i = nzi	masan(a) = i = nzi
and qpt. **me** **my**	mut. n.pl.C	**paternal** mut. n.pl.C	**gods** mut. n.pl.C

\|(LITUUS)á-za-ta
    aza = nta
they loved 3.pl.prt.

---

tatiya-, 'paternal'

☞ *tatinzi* could be analysed in two ways: 1. as an adjective 'paternal' (s. above), or 2. as a substantive 'the fathers' (analysed as *tat(a)=i=nzi* with *i*-mutation), meaning that the gods were or acted as his fathers. An interpretation as 'my paternal gods' seems more likely, and this frequently recurring phrase fits well with other expressions of continuity and dynastic claim.

☞ While the verb *a-za-ta* cannot write its plural marker of the personal ending, the preconsonantal *n*, one cannot interpret it as a singular form because the only possible subject of the clause is plural.

☞ Note the plene writing of final-*i* in DEUS-*ni-zi-i* and within the word á-*mi-i-zi*.

§ 4:   § 3:

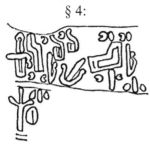   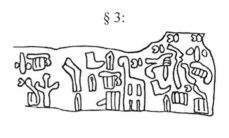

"and I settled the devastated (places),"   "and they seated me on my father's
throne,"

§ 3 |wa/i-mu-ta |á-mi |tá-ti-i |(THRONUS)i-sà-tara/i-ti-i
(a) = wa = mu = ta   ami = i   tati(ya) = i   istar(a)t(a) = i
and qpt. **me** lpt.   **my**   d.sg. **fatherly** d.sg. **on the throne** d.sg.

(SOLIUM)i-sà-nu-wa/i-ta
       isa = nuwa = nta
they seated caus. 3.pl.prt.

§ 4 |a-wa/i |("VACUUS")ta-na-ta-'   ("SOLIUM")i-sà-nu-wa/i-ha
       a = wa   tanata = a   isanuwa = ha
   conj. qpt. **the devastated (places)** a.pl.N **I settled** 1.sg.prt.

(SOLIUM)*isanuwa-*, 'to make sit; settle'   ("VACUUS")*tanata/i-*, 'devastated'
THRONUS = *istar(a)ta-* 'throne'

☞ Note the difference in meaning of *isanuwa-* 'to make sit' (caus. of *asa-* 'to
   sit') depending on whether the object is animate or not: people are 'seated'
   while regions are 'settled'.

§ 5:

"and I benefited(?) the settlements(?) by the authority of Tarhunzas and Eas."

|"SOLIUM"*(-)x-ma-ma-pa-wa/i*   (BONUS)*(-)u-su-tara/i-ha*
          = *a* = *pa* = *wa*   = *ha*
settlements(?) a.pl.N cpt. qpt.   **I benefited(?)**   1.sg.prt.

(DEUS)TONITRUS-*hu-ta-sá-ti-i*   (DEUS)*i-ia-sa-ti-ha*
     Tarhunta = *asa* = *ati*   *iya* = *asa* = *ati* = *ha*
of Tarhunzas   p.adj.   abl.   **and of Ea**s   p.adj.   abl.   cpt.

LEPUS+*ra/i-ia-ti*
       *tapariya = *ati*
by the authority   abl.

"SOLIUM"(-)*x-ma-ma*-, 'settlements(?)'   (DEUS)*Iya*-, 'Ea' [DN]
(BONUS)(-)*u-su-tara/i*-, 'to benefit(?)'   LEPUS = **tapariya*-, 'authority'
(DEUS)TONITRUS, 'Tarhunzas' [DN]

☞ As the interpretation of the sign immediately following SOLIUM is not clear
   (possibly *ri+i*?), it is transliterated *x*.

☞ Even though the underlying word is not clear, an interpretation of
   |"SOLIUM"*(-)x-ma-ma-pa-wa/i* as 'settlements' is attractive because of the
   context and the fact that SOLIUM is known as a determinative of the verb
   isanuwa-, 'to settle'.

✎ Read the entire text and check whether you have understood it.

1. § 1a EGO-*wa/i-mi-i* ᴵTONITRUS.*HALPA-pa-ru-* "I (am) Halparuntiyas,
        ti-i-ia-sa |("IUDEX")*tara/i-wa/i-ni-sà* the ruler, Gurgumean
        |*ku+ra/i-ku-ma-wa/i-ni-i-sà*(URBS) REX- king,
        ti-i-sa

   § 1b ᴵ*la+ra/i+a-ma-si-i-sa* |LEPUS+*ra/i-ia-li-i-* the son of Laramas
        sa |INFANS-*mu-wa/i-za-sà* the governor,

2. § 1c ᴵTONITRUS.*HALPA-pa-ru-ti-ia-si-sà* || grandson of the hero
        HEROS-*li-sa* |(INFANS.NEPOS)*ha-ma-* Halparuntiyas,
        si-sá-'

   § 1d *mu-wa/i-ta-li-si-sà* |("SCALPRUM+*RA/I.* great-grandson of the
        LA/I/U")*wa/i+ra/i-pa-li-sa* brave Muwatalis,
        |(INFANS.NEPOS)*ha-ma-su-ka-la-sá*

3. § 1e ᴵTONITRUS.*HALPA-pa-*CERVUS₂-*ti-ia-si-* great-great-grandson
        sà |("IUDEX")*tara/i-wa/i-ni-sá* || of the ruler
        |(INFANS)*na-wa/i-sa* Halparuntiyas,

   § 1f ᴵ*mu-wa/i-zi-si* HEROS-*li-sà* |(INFANS)*na-* great-great-great-
        wa/i-na-wa/i-sá grandson of the hero
                                                    Muwizis,

   § 1g ᴵ*la+ra/i+a-ma-si-sá* LEPUS+*ra/i-ia-li-sa* descendant of the
        |(INFANS)*ha+ra/i-tu-sá* governor Laramas."

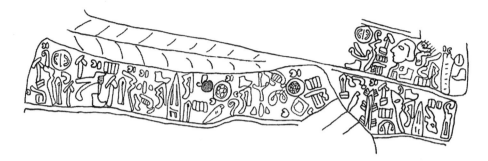

4. § 1h DEUS-*na-ti* (LITUUS)*á-za-mi-sà*
CAPUT-*ta-ti*⌈(LITUUS)⌉*u-ni-mi-sa*
|FINES-*ha-ti* || AUDIRE-*mi-sà* REX-*ti-sá*

(I am) the king loved by the gods, known by the people, heard of abroad,

§ 1i (LITUUS)*á-za-mi-sa* |(BONUS)*u-li-ia-mi-sà* |("PANIS.SCUTELLA")*mu-sa*[?]-*nu-wa/i-ti-sá* |("PANIS")*ma-li-*⌈*ri+i*⌉-*mi-i-sá* REX-*ti-sá*

the loved, exalted, satisfying(?), honey-sweet king.

§ 2 |*wa/i-mu* |*á-mi-i-zi* |*tá-ti-zi* DEUS-*ni-zi-i* |(LITUUS)*á-za-ta*

My paternal gods loved me,

§ 3 |*wa/i-mu-ta* |*á-mi* |*tá-ti-i* |(THRONUS)*i-sà-tara/i-ti-i* (SOLIUM)*i-sà-nu-wa/i-ta*

and they seated me on my father's throne.

5. § 4 |*a-wa/i* |("VACUUS")*ta-na-ta-'* ("SOLIUM")*i-sà-*||*nu-wa/i-ha*

And I settled the devastated (places),

§ 5 |"SOLIUM"(-)*x-ma-ma-pa-wa/i* (BONUS)(-)*u-su-tara/i-ha* (DEUS)TONITRUS-*hu-ta-sá-ti-i* (DEUS)*i-ia-sa-ti-ha* LEPUS+*ra/i-ia-ti*

and I benefited(?) the settlements(?) by the authority of Tarhunzas and Eas."

5.8   BOHÇA

The stele BOHÇA comes from the south-eastern Anatolian plateau, an area known to the Neo-Assyrians as Tabal. Iron Age Tabal consisted of several small city-states governed by local rulers, one of them the author of this inscription, a certain Kurtis, son of Ashwis. It is conceivable that he may be identical with Kurti of (A)tun(n)a mentioned by the Assyrian king Sargon II for the years 718 and 713 BC, thus providing an approximate date for the stele. Features such as rhotacism and the use of predominantly cursive sign forms would support such a late date. The stone, despite a reasonable state of preservation, has a rough surface and the engraving of the signs is of poor quality. It is also not certain, whether the end of line four denotes the end of the text.

The four-line inscription illustrates the ruler's intimate relationship with two gods, the Storm-God Tarhunzas and the Stag-God Runtiyas. Like many other rulers, Kurtis contrasts his situation with that of his predecessors to highlight the extent of divine preferment he experiences. The text's main theme, however, is hunting and one may wonder whether the stele was set up to express territorial claims to hunting grounds. More explicit territorial markers survive on two early orthostats from Malatya which depict hunting scenes accompanied by an epigraph naming the person to whom the shootings belong.

📖 *Edition*: Hawkins, 2000, 478–480.

§ 1:

"I (am) Kurtis, the hero Ashwis' son, the king heard of in the west and east."

EGO-*mi* [|ʔ]*ku+ra/i-ti-i-sá* |*á-⌈sa-HWI-si⌉-sa₄*
amu = mi   *kurti = s*   *ashwi =(a)s(a) = i = s*
I (am) refl.   **Kurtis** n.sg.C   **of Ashwis** p.adj. mut. n.sg.C

|HEROS-*li-i-sa* |("INFANS")*ni-mu-wa/i-za-sa*
*hastali(ya) = i = s   *nimuwiza = s*
of the hero mut. n.sg.C   **son**   n.sg.C

("OCCIDENS")*i-pa-ma-ri+i-i* |ORIENS+*MI-ma-ri+i-ha*
       ipama = ari   *kistama = ari = ha*
from the west   abl.sg.   **from the east**   abl.sg. **and**

|PRAE |AUDIRE+*MI-ti-mi-⌈sa₄⌉*||| [|]REX-*ti-sá*
paran *tuma(n)ti =(a)m(a) = i = s   **hantawat = i = s*
the heard of one   part. mut. n.sg.C   **king**   mut. n.sg.C

---

kurti-, 'Kurtis' [PN]   ORIENS = *kistama/i-*, 'east'
ashwi-, 'Ashwis, [PN]   PRAE AUDIRE = *paran *tuma(n)ti-*,
OCCIDENS = *ipama/i-*, 'west'   'to hear of'

☞ The forms *ipamari* and *kistamari* are both rhotacised forms of the ablative in
-*ati*. The function of the ablative here is very close to that of the dative,
expressing 'where' rather than 'wherefrom' the action took place. A good
translation would therefore be 'heard of in' rather than 'from', see header.

☞ Remember that *ri* attached to *i* as in |ORIENS+*MI-ma-ri+i-ha* is not
tranliterated -*i+ra/i-* but as -*ri+i-* because the vowel sign merely defines the
vocalisation of the sign *ra/i*, cf. above, 2.2. This is confirmed by plene
writing of the vowel such as *i-pa-ma-ri+i-i*.

§ 2:   § 3:

"Here I am good to   "And he grants me to take the territories over."
Tarhunzas"

§ 2 |wa/i-ta |(DEUS)TONITRUS-*hu-ti* |za-ri+i
     (a) = wa = ta   tarhunt = i   zari
     and   qpt. lpt.   **to Tarhunzas** d.sg.   **here** adv.

|(BONUS)wa/i-su-wa/i-i
     wasu = wi
I am good   1.sg.prs.

§ 3 |wa/i-mu |TERRA-REL+ra/i-zi   SUPER+ra/i
     (a) = wa = mu   *taskwir = i = nzi   sara
     and   qpt.   **to me**   **the territories** mut. a.pl.C   **over** prev.

|"CAPERE"(-)la/i/u-na-' |pi-pa-sa-i
(la)la(?) = una   pipasa = i
to take   inf.   **he grants** 3.sg.prs.

---

zari, 'here'   CAPERE = (la)la-?, 'to take'
TERRA-REL = *taskwira/i-, 'land,   pipasa-, v.iter. of piya-, 'to give'
territory'

☞ The adverb *zari* is rhotacised from original *zati*.
☞ The verb *pipasa* shows iteration twice, through reduplication as well as
   through the iterative suffix -sa. Contrast this form with *pipasaya* in the
   closely parallel clause § 9. Both are 3.sg.prs. but the present form has the
   shorter ending -i.

§ 4:   § 5:

"Here I am good to Runtiyas"   "And here he gives to me wild
                                        animals for shooting."

§ 4 |(DEUS)CERVUS₂-ti-pa-wa/i-ta-' |za-ri+i(-)ia(-)pa-'
          runti = i = pa = wa = ta   zari   ?   ?
       to Runtiyas d.sg. cpt. qpt. lpt.   **here**

|(BONUS)wa/i-su-wa/i   § 5 |wa/i-mu |za-ri+i
   wasu = wi   (a) = wa = mu   zari
I am good 1.sg.prs.   **and** qpt. **to me**   **here**

|sà-ma-ia |("ANIMAL.BESTIA")HWI-sa₅+ra/i |pi-pa-sa-ia
    sa = ma = ia   hwisar = a   pipasa = ia
for shooting v.noun d.sg. **wild animals** a.pl.N   **he gives** 3.sg.prs.

---

wasu-, 'to be good'   (ANIMAL.BESTIA)hwisar-, hwitar-,
sa-, 'press, seal; shoot'   'wild animal'

☞ The translation of § 4 omits the connective particle -pa 'but, and' because in
   English it would be rather tedious to begin every clause with 'and'.
☞ |za-ri+i-ia-pa-': because of the parallel clause § 2, we can identify zari but
   the sequence (-)ia(-)pa-' remains unclear.
☞ For deverbal nouns in -ma/i- cf. above, 3.1.1.1.
☞ The Procida acts set out a reading LEO (for BESTIA), and CERVUS₃ (for
   CERVUS₂), s. sign list. The CHLI readings have been kept here to facilitate
   cross-reference with the edition.

§ 7:   § 6:

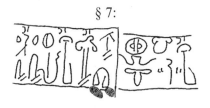   

"indeed Tarhunzas did not help (them)   "And (those) who were my fathers and
at all,"   grandfathers,"

§ 6 |á-mi-zi-pa-wa/i |tá-ti-zi-i |AVUS-ha-zi-ha
     am(a) = i = nzi = pa = wa   tat(a) = i = nzi   huha = nzi = ha
     my   mut. n.pl.C **and** qpt. **fathers** mut. n.pl.C **grandfathers** n.pl.C **and**

|REL-zi   [|á-]sa-ta
kwi = nzi   asa = nta
who   n.pl.C   **they were** 3.pl.prt.

§ 7 |REL-pa-wa/i   (DEUS)TONITRUS-hu-za-sa |NEG₂ |REL-ha-na
       kwipa = wa   Tarhunza = s   na kwihan
       indeed   qpt.   **Tarhunzas** n.sg.C   **not at all**

|wa/i+ra/i-ia-ia
  wariya = ia
he helped   3.sg.prs.

AVUS = huha-, 'grandfather'   na kwihan, 'not at all'
REL-pa = kwipa, 'indeed'   wariya-, 'to help'

☞ While § 7 clearly refers to the past, the verb *wariyaya* is present. Such a
'historical present' is used as a lively representation of the past, cf. 4.7.2.
Note that the closely parallel clause § 11 has a preterite verb.

§ 9:   § 8:

"He grants me to take over the   "as he helps me."
            territories."

§ 8 |á-mu-wa/i |REL+ra/i |wa/i+ra/i-ia-ia
     amu = wa   kwari   wariya = ia
     me qpt.   **as**   **he helps** 3.sg.prs.

§ 9 |wa/i-mu |"TERRA"-REL+ra/i-zi   SUPER+ra/i
     (a) = wa = mu   taskwir = i = nzi   sara
     conj. qpt. **me** **territories** mut. a.pl.C   **over**   prev.

|"CAPERE"(-)la/i/u-na |pi-pa-sa-ia
(la)la(?) = una   pipasa = ia
   to take   inf.   **he grants** 3.sg.prs.

REL+ra/i = kwari, 'as'   SUPER+ra/i CAPERE = sara (la)la-, 'to
                                  take over'

☞ Compare §§ 9 and 3. Save for a few orthographic differences the clauses are
   identical.

§ 10:

§ 11:

"And when my fathers and grandfathers went riding sometime(?),"

"indeed Runtiyas did not help (them) at all,"

§ 10 |*á-mi-zi-ha* |*tá-ti-zi* || AVUS-*ha-zi-ha-*$^{?}$ |REL-*i*
    am(a) = i = nzi = ha   *tat(a) = i = nzi*   *huha = nzi = ha*   *kwi*
    my mut. n.pl.C **and fathers** mut. n.pl.C **and grandfathers   when**

"ANIMAL.EQUUS<">-*zú-sà-ta-la-u-na*   REL   "PES$_2$.PES$_2$"(-)*tà-ta*
azusantala = una   indef.?   *ta(?) = nta*
    to ride inf.   **sometime(?) they went** 3.pl.prt.

§ 11 |REL-*pa-wa/i*   (DEUS)CERVUS$_2$-*ti-ia-*⌈*sá*$^{?}$⌉   [|$^{?}$]NEG$_2$-'   [|$^{?}$]REL-*ha-na*
    kwipa = wa   *Runtiya = s*   *nawa   kwihan*
    indeed   qpt.   **Runtiyas**   n.sg.C   **not at all**

[|$^{?}$]*wa/i+ra/i*[-*ia*$^{?}$]-*ta*
  wariya = ta
he helped 3.sg.prt.

REL-*i = kwi*, 'when'   REL = whenever(?)
ANIMAL.EQUUS = *azusantala-*, 'to   PES$_2$.PES$_2$ = *ta-*, 'to go'
ride'

☞ Note the position of REL-*i*, 'when', following the subject. The function of the second relative is not entirely clear; possibly indefinite?

☞ The infinitive *azusantalauna* is dependent on the predicate 'they went'. *azusantala-* can be analysed as a denominative verb in *-al-* of a composite noun *azu(wa)-* 'horse' + intransitive *asant(i)-* 'sitting' (participle of *asa-*, 'sit, dwell') with the sense '(one who is) sitting-on-a-horse, riding = rider'. We therefore arrive at a meaning 'to ride' for the verb *azusantala-*.[36]

36 See Neumann, 2004.

§ 12:   § 13:

"as he helps me:"   "and in this territory, in this place I took 100 gazelles at
                                   one time(?) since(?) ..."

§ 12   [|?]á-*mu-wa/i* |REL+*ra/i* |*wa/i+ra/i-ia-ia*
           amu = wa   *kwari*   *wariya = ia*
           me   qpt.   **as**   **he helps**   3.sg.prs.

§ 13 |[*a*?]-*wa/i* |*za-ti-i* |"TERRA"-*sa*-REL+*ra/i-i* |*za-ti-i*
           a = wa   *zat = i*   *taskwira = i*   *zat = i*
           and qpt.   **in this** d.sg.   **territory**   d.sg.   **in this** d.sg.

|LOCUS-*ta₅-ti-i*   1 x CENTUM   (ANIMAL)GAZELLA   *la-ha*
pitant = i   *irwa = nzi*   *la = ha*
place   d.sg.   100   **gazelles**   a.pl.C   **I took** 1.sg.prt.

"UNUS?"-*ta* |REL-*za*   ...
                             kwa(n)za
once   **since(?)**

(ANIMAL)GAZELLA = *irwa-*,   REL-*za* = *kwa(n)za*, 'since'
'gazelle' UNUS-*ta*, 'once'

☞ The Procida reading of GAZELLA is CAPRA, cf. sign list, *104.

☞ The form of "UNUS?"-*ta* is unclear, -*ta* most likely expresses multiplication
   'once', cf. above, 3.3. A translation 'at one time' would fit the context even
   better if we take this clause as illustrating how great the author's deeds were
   because of divine favour.

☞ As the text breaks off here, one cannot be sure whether REL-*za* belongs to
   this or the following clause.

☞ For LOCUS-*ta₅*- cf. also Rieken–Yakubovich 2010: 208–210.

➤ Read the entire text and check whether you have understood it.

1. § 1   EGO-*mi* [|*²*]*ku+ra/i-ti-i-sa* |*á-⌈sa-HWI-si⌉-sa₄*   "I (am) Kurtis, the
          |HEROS-*li-i-sa* |("INFANS")*ni-mu-wa/i-za-*   hero Ashwis' son,
          sa ("OCCIDENS")*i-pa-ma-ri+i-i*   the king heard of in
2. |ORIENS+*MI-ma-ri+i-ha* |PRAE   the west and in the
          |AUDIRE+*MI-ti-mi-⌈sa₄⌉* || [|]REX-*ti-sá*   east.
   § 2 |*wa/i-ta* |(DEUS)TONITRUS-*hu-ti* |*za-ri+i*   And here I am good
          |(BONUS)*wa/i-su-wa/i-i*   to Tarhunzas,
   § 3 |*wa/i-mu* |TERRA-REL+*ra/i-zi* SUPER+*ra/i*   and he grants me to
          |"CAPERE"(-)*la/i/u-na-'* |*pi-pa-sa-i*   take over the
                                                               territories,
   § 4 |(DEUS)CERVUS₂-*ti-pa-wa/i-ta-'* |*za-ri+i*   but here I am good
          (-)*ia(-)pa-'* |(BONUS)*wa/i-su-wa/i*   to Runtiyas,
   § 5 |*wa/i-mu* |*za-ri+i* |*sà-ma-ia* || and here he gives
          ("ANIMAL.BESTIA")HWI-*sa₅+ra/i* |*pi-pa-*   wild animals for
          sa-ia   shooting to me.
3. § 6 |*á-mi-zi-pa-wa/i* |*tá-ti-zi-i* |AVUS-*ha-zi-ha*   And (those) who
          |REL-*zi* [|?]*sa-ta*   were my fathers and
                                                               grandfathers,

§ 7	|REL-*pa-wa/i* (DEUS)TONITRUS-*hu-za-sa* |NEG₂ |REL-*ha-na* |*wa/i+ra/i-ia-ia*	indeed Tarhunzas did not help (them) at all,
§ 8	|*á-mu-wa/i* |REL+*ra/i* |*wa/i+ra/i-ia-ia*	as he helps me:
§ 9	|*wa/i-mu* |"TERRA"-REL+*ra/i-zi* SUPER+*ra/i* |"CAPERE"(-)*la/i/u-na* |*pi-pa-sa-ia*	he grants me to take over the territories.
4. § 10	|*á-mi-zi-ha* |*tá-ti-zi* || AVUS-*ha-zi-ha-'* ⌜?⌝ |REL-*i* "ANIMAL.EQUUS<">-*zú-sà-ta-la-u-na* REL "PES₂.PES₂"(-)*tà-ta*	And when my fathers and grandfathers went riding sometime(?),
§ 11	|REL-*pa-wa/i* (DEUS)CERVUS₂-*ti-ia*-⌜*sá*?⌝ [|?]NEG₂-' [|?]REL-*ha-na* [|?]*wa/i+ra/i*[-*ia*?]-*ta*	indeed Runtiyas did not help (them) at all,
§ 12	[|?]*á-mu-wa/i* |REL+*ra/i* |*wa/i+ra/i-ia-ia*	as he helps me.
§ 13	|[*á*?]-*wa/i* |*za-ti-i* |"TERRA"-*sa*-REL+*ra/i-i* |*za-ti-i* |LOCUS-*ta₅-ti-i* 1 x CENTUM (ANIMAL)GAZELLA *la-ha* "UNUS?"-*ta* |REL-*za* ...	And in this territory, in this place I took 100 gazelles at one time(?) since(?)..."

5.9   KARKAMIŠ A11b+c

Two portal orthostats, A11b+c, preserve a building inscription of the ruler Katuwas (cf. text 5). The inscription runs in six lines across orthostat A11b, then similarly across A11c and begins, as we would expect, with the author's genealogy. A summary of historical events preceding the building activity follows, informing us of a revolt in Karkamiš which Katuwas succefully put down.

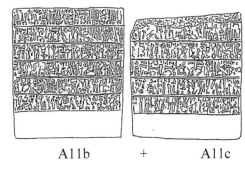

A11b   +   A11c

Not surprisingly, he claims that divine preferment and aid lead to military success. All of this is the reason for Katuwas' thank-offering, namely the building of upper floors to the city gates as women's quarters, as well as a procession for his main gods, Karhuhas and Kubabas, and various sacrifices. Damage to the top of A11c induces a short gap in the narrative, the text continues with an elaborate protective curse formula and a summary of the lead theme, the building of women's quarters for his wife. The following excerpt of the long inscription begins with Katuwas' illustration of the gods' love for him, followed by cultic stipulations and the main part of the protective curse.

📖 *Edition*: Hawkins, 2000, 101–108.

§ 9:

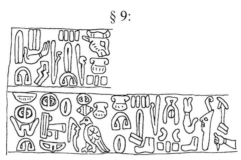

"But because of my justice my lord, celestial Tarhunzas, Karhuhas and Kubabas
loved me."

mu-pa-wa/i-*a	*mi-i-sa-*a*	DOMINUS-*na-ní-sa* ‖
amu = pa = wa	*am(a) = i = s*	*= s*
me **but** qpt.	**my** mut. n.sg.C	**lord** n.sg.C

CAELUM	(DEUS)TONITRUS-*sa*	(DEUS)*kar-hu-ha-sá*
tipas = as(a) = i = s	*tarhunza = s*	*karhuha = s*
of the sky p.adj. mut. n.sg.C	**Tarhunzas** n.sg.C	**Karhuhas** n.sg.C

(DEUS)*ku+AVIS-pa-pa-sa-ha*	*mi-ia-ti-*a*	"IUSTITIA"-*wa/i-na-ti*
kubaba = s = ha	*amiya = ati*	*tarwan(a) = ati*
Kubabas n.sg.C **and**	**because of my** abl.sg.	**justice** abl.sg.

(LITUUS)*á-za-tá*
    aza = nta
they loved   3.pl.prt.

CAELUM = *tipas-*, 'sky'   IUSTITIA = *tarwan(a)-*, 'justice'
(DEUS)*karhuha-*, 'Karhuhas' [DN]

☞ Tarhunzas, Karhuhas and Kubabas head the local pantheon at Karkamiš.
☞ Many rulers cite *amiyati tarwanati* 'because of my justice' as the reason why
    the gods treated them particularly well. For the ablative expressing cause, cf.
    above, 4.2.5.

§ 10:

"for me they sat on the HUHURPALI"

§ 11:

"they ran before me."

§ 10   *wa/i-ma-tá-*a*   ("LIGNUM")*hu-hú+ra/i-pa-li* |(SOLIUM)*á-sa-tá*
        a = wa = mu = ata   *huhurpali = i*   *asa = nta*
        and qpt. **for me they** **on the HUHURPALI**   d.sg.   **they sat**   3.pl.prt.

§ 11   *wa/i-ma-tà-*a* |PRAE-*na*   (PES₂)*HWI-ia-ta*
        a = wa = mu = ata   *paran*   *hwiya = nta*
        and qpt.   **me**   **they**   **before**   **they ran**   3.pl.prt.

(LIGNUM)*huhurpali-*, '?'   *apa-*, 'this'
(SOLIUM)*asa-*, 'to sit'   (VACUUS)*tanata-*, 'to waste'
(PES₂)*hwiya-*, 'to run'

☞ (LIGNUM)*huhurpali-* is only attested here. LIGNUM appears elsewhere as a determinative of wooden objects and of terms denoting authority. Because of the verb *asa-*, one could expect *huhurpali-* to be a concrete object rather than an abstract term. Melchert interprets it as a part of the war chariot, possibly a round shield mounted on it, named because of its similar shape after the Hittite musical instrument ᴳᴵˢ*hu(wa)hu(r)pal(li)-*, 'clapper'.[37] This would provide a good sense for the above sentence, as it evokes a vivid picture of the gods sitting on Katuwas' war chariot, i.e. actively supporting his cause. The following clause which tells us that the gods ran before the king - a very common topos of divine preferment - would support this interpretation; one may certainly expect a successul outcome of the enterprise.

---

37 1988, 229. But see also Rieken, 1999, 452–4.

§ 12:   § 13:

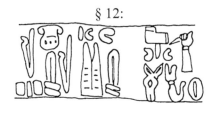   

"And I wasted these lands"   "and the trophies? I brought inside."

§ 12   *a-wa/i*   *pa-ia-*a* |REGIO-*ni-ia*   ("VACUUS")*ta-na-tá-ha*
       a = wa   *apa = ia*   *utni = ia*   *tanata = ha*
       and qpt. **these** a.pl.N **lands** a.pl.N   **I wasted** 1.sg.prt.

§ 13   *wa/i-ta-*a*   (SCALPRUM.CAPERE₂)*u-pa-ní-zi*   *a-tá*
       a = wa = ta   *upan(a) = i = nzi*   *anta*
       and qpt. lpt.   **the trophies**?   mut. a.pl.C   **inside**

|("CAPERE₂")‖*u-pa-ha*
    upa = ha
I brought 1.sg.prt.

(SCALPRUM.CAPERE₂)*upana/i-*,   ("CAPERE₂")*upa-*, 'to bring'
'trophies?'

☞ The determinative SCALPRUM is used for stone objects, CAPERE for the
verb *upa-*, 'to bring' from which the above noun *upani-* seems to derive. An
interpretation of these brought-in objects as trophies would fit the context.

§ 15:

§ 14:

"These upper floors? I built myself in that year."

"and I came up glorified from those lands."

§ 14	a-wa/i	pi-i-na-*a	|REGIO-ni-ia-ti	(FULGUR)pi-ha-mi-sa
	a = wa	apin	*utni = ati	piham(a) = i = s
	and qpt.	**from those**	**lands** abl.pl.	**glorified** mut. n.sg.C

SUPER+ra/i-'	|PES-wa/i-i-ha
sara	awi = ha
up	**I came** 1.sg.prt.

§ 15	|za-zi-ha-wa/i-mi-i			(DOMUS.SUPER)ha+ra/i-sà-tá-ni-zi
	za = nzi = ha = wa = mi			haristan(a) = i = nzi
	these a.pl.C **and** qpt. **myself**			**upper floors?** mut. a.pl.C

pa-ti-i-*a	("ANNUS")u-si	|AEDIFICARE-MI-ha
apat = i	us(a) = i	tama = ha
in that d.sg.	**year** d.sg.	**I built** 1.sg.prt.

---

pihama/i-, 'glorified'   ANNUS = usa/i-, 'year'
(DOMUS.SUPER)haristana/i-, 'upper
floors?'

☞ pihama/i- is a denominative adjective of the noun *piha-, 'lightning, glory, might', literally 'imbued with splendour'. It is a common epithet of the Storm-God.

☞ The double determinative DOMUS.SUPER points towards an interpretation of the word haristana/i- as 'upper floors'. We learn from other Katuwas inscriptions that these upper floors were build as women's quarters for his wife Anas (KARKAMIŠ A11a, § 19) and were located at the gate (KARKAMIŠ A11b+c, §34).

§ 16:

"And I saw the procession of my lord Karhuhas and Kubabas for myself,"

wa/i-mi-ta-*a	mi-i-na-*a	DOMINUS-na-i-ni-i-na
a = wa = mi = ta	am(a) = i = n	= n
and qpt. **for myself** lpt.	**my** mut. a.sg.C	**lord** a.sg.C

(DEUS)kar-hu-ha-si-na	(DEUS)ku+AVIS-pa-si-ha
Karhuha = as(a) = i = n	kubaba = as(a) = i = n = ha
of Karhuhas p.adj. mut. a.sg.C	**of Kubabas** p.adj. mut. a.sg.C **and**

CRUS.CRUS(-)ní-ia-sa-ha-na	|LITUUS+na-ha
niyasha = n	*mana(?) = ha
the procession a.sg.C	**I saw** 1.sg.prt.

CRUS.CRUS(-)niyasha-, 'procession'   LITUUS = *mana-(?), 'to see'

☞ The suffix -sha- forms a deverbal noun niyasha- 'procession' from the verb (ni)ni(ya)-, 'to lead, follow'. Cf. above, 3.1.1.1.

☞ The logogram LITUUS is the determinative of verbs of seeing, further aza-, 'to love' and uni-, 'to know'. Hieroglyphic Luwian does not preserve a phonetic writing for LITUUS-na but Cuneiform Luwian has mana-, 'to see'.

§ 17:

§ 18a:

"and I seated them on this podium,"

"and the sacrifice for them (shall be) this: with the gods annual bread,"

§ 17   *wa/i-ma-tá-*a* |*za*||*-ti-i* |("PODIUM")*hu-ma-ti*
        a = wa = mu = ata   *zat = i*   *humt = i*
        and qpt. **I** **them** **on this** d.sg. **podium** d.sg.

|(SOLIUM)*i-sà-nú-wa/i-ha*
    isa = nuwa = ha
I made sit caus.   1.sg.prt.

§ 18a ("*350")*á-sa-ha+ra/i-mi-sà-pa-wa/i-ma-za* |*za-'*
        asharmis = a = pa = wa = manza   *za = ∅*
        the sacrifice n.pl.N **and** qpt. **for them**   **this** n.sg.N

DEUS-*ní-za* |CUM-*ni*   ANNUS-*sa-li-za-sa* |("PANIS")*tú+ra/i-pi-sa*
masani = (a)nza   *usaliza = s*   *turp(a) = i = s*
gods d.pl.   **with**   **annual** n.sg.C   **bread** mut. n.sg.C

(PODIUM)*humt(i)-*, 'podium'   *asharmis-*, 'sacrifice[?]'
ashar-, 'blood'   *-manza*, 'for them'

☞ § 18a: remember that the particle chain is added to any initial accented word.
☞ For *asharmis-* as a neuter stem in *–is-*, cf. Melchert, 2004b, 472–3.

§ 18b: § 18c:

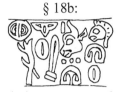

"for Karhuhas, one ox and sheep,"   "for Kubabas, an ox and a sheep,"

§ 18b   (DEUS)CERVUS₂+ra/i-hu-ha-ia   1   BOS(ANIMAL)-sa
         karhuha = ia   *waw(a) = i = s*
         for Karhuhas d.sg.   **one**   **ox**   mut. n.sg.C

OVIS-*sa-ha*
haw(a) = i = s
sheep   mut. n.sg.C

§ 18c   (DEUS)*ku*+AVIS-*pa-pa*   1   BOS(ANIMAL)-*sa*   1
         kubaba = a   *waw(a) = i = s*
         for Kubabas d.sg.   **one**   **ox**   mut. n.sg.C   **one**

OVIS(ANIMAL)-*wa/i-sa-ha*
haw(a) = i = s = ha
sheep   mut. n.sg.C   **and**

OVIS = *hawa/i-*, 'sheep'

☞ ANIMAL functions as a postdeterminative to BOS and OVIS. But as you
can see in § 18b, it is not always used consistently.

§ 18d:

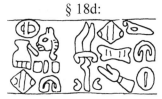

§ 18e:

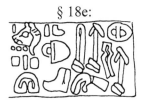

"for the god Sarkus a sheep and a
KUTUPILIS,"

"one sheep for the male gods,"

§ 18d	(DEUS)sa₅+ra/i-ku	OVIS-wa/i-sa	("*478")ku-tú-pi-li-sa-ha
	sarku = ∅	haw(a) = i = s	kutupili = s = ha
	for Sarkus d.sg.	**sheep** mut. n.sg.C	**KUTUPILI** n.sg.C **and**

§ 18e	1	OVIS(ANIMAL)wa/i-sa	|VIR-ti-ia-tà-za	DEUS-ní-za ||
		haw(a) = i = s	zitiyant = anza	masani = (a)nza
	one	**sheep** mut. n.sg.C	**male** d.pl.	**for the gods** d.pl.

(*478)kutupili-, 'lamb(?)'   zitiyant(i)-, 'male'
sarku-, 'mighty one'

☞ sarku- is attested in Hittite with the meaning 'exalted, mighty'. An epithet of
the god Eas, it appears here instead of the god's name.

☞ As all offerings of this sentence have mentioned the bigger item first, one
may conclude that a kutupili- must be worth less than a sheep. Could it be a
young lamb or another small animal?

§ 18f: § 19:

"[one she]ep for the fe[male   "[... Wh]o(?) approaches
gods]"   these [gods] with badness,"

§ 18f [1 OVIS(ANIMAL-*wa/i*]-*sa* [FEMINA-*ti*]-*ia*-[*ta*]-*za* [DEUS-*ni*-*za*]
        haw(a) = *i* = *s*   *wanatiyant* = *anza*   *masani* = *(a)nza*
        one sheep mut. n.sg.C   **female**   d.pl.   **for the gods** d.pl.

§ 19   [... REL]-*sa*   *z*[*a*-*ti*]-*ia*-*za*   [DEUS-*n*]*i*$^?$-*za*
       [... *kwi*] = *s*   *zati* = *anza*   *masani* = *(a)nza*
       [Who]   n.sg.C **to these** d.pl.   **gods**   d.pl.

MALUS-*ta₄*-*ti*-*i*-' ‖   VERSUS-*ia*-*ni* |PES-*wa/i*-*ti*
    haniyata = *ati*   *tawiyani*   *awi* = *ti*
with badness abl.sg.   **towards**   **he comes** 3.sg.prs.

---

wanatiyant(i)-, 'female'   VERSUS = *tawiyan(i)*, 'towards'
MALUS = *haniyata*-, 'badness'

☞ Unfortunately, the top line of the orthostat A11c is damaged. § 18f can be
  easily restored as one would expect it to be closely parallel to the preceding
  clause. While we cannot be sure of the content of the lost section, it must
  have contained either further sacrifical regulations or the beginning of the
  protective curse. § 19 belongs to the 'if' stipulations of the curse, the
  protasis.

☞ For MALUS-*ta₄*- cf. also Rieken–Yakubovich 2010: 202.

§ 21:   § 20

"or if it shall pass down to   "or comes towards these upper floors? with
        (someone),"   badness,"

§ 20 |NEG₂-*pa-wa/i-sa* |*za-ti-ia-za*   (DOMUS.SUPER)*ha+ra/i-sà-tá-na-za*
        napa = wa = as   *zati = anza*   *haristana = anza*
        or   qpt. **he** **to these** d.pl.   **upper floors?** d.pl.

MALUS-*ta₄-ti-i-'* |VERSUS-*ia-ni* [PES]-*wa/i-ti*
     haniyata = ati   *tawiyani*   *awi = ti*
  with badness abl.sg. **towards**   **he comes** 3.sg.prs.

§ 21   [|]NEG₂-[*pa*]-*wa/i-tà*   CRUS.CRUS[(-)*ni*²]-*ia-za-i*   REL-*a-ti*
        napa = wa = ta   *niya = za = i*   *kwati*
        or   qpt. lpt.   **it shall pass down** iter. 3.sg.prs. **if**

PRAE-*na*
paran
prev.

NEG₂-*pa = napa*, 'or'   *kwati*, 'if'
CRUS.CRUS(-)*niyaza-*, 'pass'(?)

☞ For the disjunctive NEG₂-*pa*, cf. above, 4.11.4.
☞ The context suggests a meaning of 'pass down to someone' for
  CRUS.CRUS(-)*niyazai* PRAE-*na* (lit. 'lead (to) before (someone)'). The
  unmentioned 'someone' may be found in REL-*i-sa* of the following clause.
☞ Note the unusual position of the preverb at the end of the clause.

§ 23:   § 22:

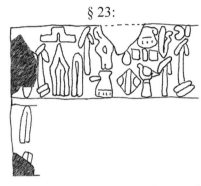   

"and [overthr]ows these orthostats in   "who takes(?) them/it ...,"
        their places,"

§ 22   [wa/i]-tà-*a   [SCRIBA+RA/I](-)tà-⌈i⌉   [||]REL-i-sa
        a = wa = ata   ...   ta = i (?)   kwi = s
        and qpt. **them/it ...**   **he takes** 3.sg.prs.   **who**   n.sg.C.

§ 23 |za-a-zi-pa-wa/i-tá   [(SCALPRUM)]ku-ta-sa₅+ra/i-zi-i
        za = nzi = pa = wa = ta   kutasar(a) = i = nzi
        these a.pl.C **but**   qpt. lpt. **orthostats**   mut. a.pl.C

LOCUS-ta₄-za   [(SA₄)sá-n]i̥||-i-t[i]
        *pida = ant = anza   sani = ti
in their places   suff.   d.pl. **he overthrows** 3.sg.prs.

(SCALPRUM)kutasara/i-, 'orthostats'   (SA₄)sani-, 'to overthrow'

☞ § 23 is restored on the basis of a parallel clause in another Katuwas
    inscription (KARKAMIŠ A11a, § 22). SCRIBA+RA/I seems to stand for a
    word connected with 'writing' - maybe *gulzattar 'writing (surface)(?)' -
    suggesting a sense 'if anyone takes my orthostat and writes his own
    inscription on it' for this clause.[38]
☞ 'in their places': the possessive is not written but may be understood here.
☞ For LOCUS-ta₄ cf. also Rieken–Yakubovich 2010: 208–210.

38 Cf. Starke, 1990, 463-4.

§ 24:

"or erases my name on these orthostats,"

|NEG₂-*pa-wa/i-tá*	|*za-a-ti-ia-za*	|("SCALPRUM")*ku-ta-sa₅+ra/i-za*
napa = wa = ta	*zati = anza*	*kutasara = anza*
or qpt. lpt.	**on these** d.pl.	**orthostats** d.pl.

|*á-ma-za*	|*á-ta₅-ma-za*	|*ARHA*	|"MALLEUS"-*la/i/u-i*
ama = an = za	*ataman = ∅ = za*	*arha*	*= i*
my a.sg.N npt.	**name** a.sg.N npt.	**he erases**	3.sg.prs.

---

arha MALLEUS, 'to destroy
completely; erase'

☞ Many inscriptions contain a curse in case anyone should erase the author's name. A realistic fear, as such *damnatio memoriae* was widely practised in the ancient world. The Egyptians, for instance, believed that erasing a person's name denied his existence on earth and therefore denied him access to the next world.

25:

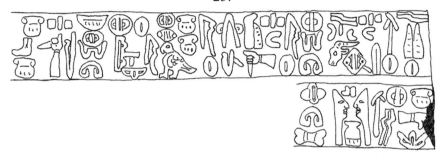

"against him let the celestial Tarhunzas, Karhuhas and Kubabas, the Storm-god of the Arputaean mountain and the Sakuraean gods of the river-land litigate!"

pa-ti-pa-wa/i-tá-*a   CAELUM
    apat = i = pa = wa = ta   *tipas = as(a) = i = s*
against him d.sg. **but** qpt. lpt. **of the sky** p.adj. mut. n.sg.C

(DEUS)TONITRUS-*sa* (DEUS)*kar-hu-ha-sá* (DEUS)*ku+*AVIS-*pa-pa-sá-ha*
Tarhunza = s   *Karhuha = s*   *Kubaba = s = ha*
Tarhunzas n.sg.C   **Karhuhas** n.sg.C   **Kubabas** n.sg.C **and**

(MONS)*a+ra/i-pu-tá-wa/i-ni-sá-ha*   (DEUS)TONITRUS-*sa*
    arputa = wan = i = s = ha   *Tarhunza = s*
the Arputaean mountain eth. mut. n.sg.C **and**   **Tarhunzas** n.sg.C

("FLUMEN+MINUS")*sà-ku+ra/i-wa/i-ni-i-zi-ha*   (FLUMEN.REGIO)*ha||-pa-tà-si*
    sakura = wan = i = nzi = ha   *hapat = asi*
the Sakurawaean eth. mut. n.pl.C **and**   **river-land** g.sg.

DEUS-*ní-zi* |LIS-*la/i/u-sa-tú*
masan(a) = i = nzi   = *antu*
gods   mut. n.pl.C **let them litigate!** 3.pl.imp.

(MONS)*arputa-*, 'Arputa' [GN]   LIS-*la/i/u-*, 'to litigate'
("FLUMEN+MINUS")*sakura-*,
       'Sakura' [GN]

§ 27:   § 26:

"(or) let them sever? her femininity,"   "Let them sever? his masculinity,"

§ 26   *wa/i-tú-*a* |VIR-*ti-ia-ti-ia-za-ha*
       a = wa = tu   *zitiyantiya = n = za = ha*
       and qpt. **for him masculinity** a.sg.N npt.   cpt.

|("CULTER")*pa+ra/i-tú-ní-tú-u*
       partuni = ntu
let them sever? 3.pl.imp.

§ 27   FEMINA-*ti-ia-ti-ia-za-ha-wa/i-tú-u* |("CULTER")*pa+ra/i-tú-ni-i-tú*
       wanatiyatiya = n = za = ha = wa = tu   *partuni = ntu*
       femininity   a.sg.N npt. **and**   qpt. **for her**   **let them sever?** 3.pl.imp.

---

zitiyantiya-, 'masculinity'   *wanatiyantiya*-, 'femininity'
(CULTER)*partuni*-, 'sever?'

☞ The verb *partuni*- is unknown, but its determinative CULTER occurs in other inscriptions with the verb 'to cut', thus suggesting a similar action here - certainly a severe punishment!

☞ Because of its common gender, the enclitic pronoun -*tu* can mean both 'for him' and 'for her'.

☞ For the possessive contruction ('his masculinity', 'her femininity') with the dative personal pronoun s. above, 4.2.3.

§ 29:

§ 28:

"(or) take to her female seed!"   "they shall not take to him male seed,"

§ 28   *wa/i-tú-*a* |VIR-*ti-ia-ti-i-na* |(*462)*mu-wa/i-i-tà-na*
       a = wa = tu   *zitiyant = i = n*   *muwita = n*
       and qpt. **to him**   **male**   mut. a.sg.C   **seed**   a.sg.C

NEG₃-*sa* |*tà-ti-i*
nis   *ta = nti*
not   **let them take**   3.pl.prs.

§ 29   FEMINA-*ti-i[a]-ti-pa-wa/i-tú*   (FEMINA.*462)‖4?-*tà* |*ni-i*
       wanatiyant = i = n = pa = wa = tu   *muwita(?)*   *ni*
       female   mut. a.sg.C **but**   qpt. **to her**   **seed** a.sg.C (n.e.)   **not**

|*tà-ti-i*
             ta = nti
let them take   3.pl.prs.

(*462)*muwita-*, 'seed'   *ni*, 'not'
(FEMINA.*462)‖4?-*tà* = *muwita-(?)*

☞ A negative command such as 'let them not take' is expressed the present
   indicative (iussive), not with the imperative; cf. above, 4.7.3.

📖 Read the entire text and check whether you have understood it.

§ 9	*mu-pa-wa/i-*a mi-i-sa-*a* DOMINUS-*na-ní-sa* ‖ CAELUM (DEUS)TONITRUS-*sa* (DEUS)*kar-hu-ha-sá* (DEUS)*ku*+AVIS-*pa-pa-sa-ha mi-ia-ti-*a* "IUSTITIA"-*wa/i-na-ti* (LITUUS)*á-za-tá*	But because of my justice my lord, celestial Tarhunzas, Karhuhas and Kubabas loved me.
§ 10	*wa/i-ma-tá-*a* ("LIGNUM")*hu-hú+ra/i-pa-li* ‖(SOLIUM)*á-sa-tá*	For me they sat on the HUHURPALI
§ 11	*wa/i-ma-tá-*a* |PRAE-*na* (PES₂)HWI-*ia-ta*	they ran before me.
§ 12	*a-wa/i pa-ia-*a* |REGIO-*ni-ia* ("VACUUS")*ta-na-tá-ha*	And I wasted the lands,
§ 13	*wa/i-ta-*a* (SCALPRUM.CAPERE₂)*u-pa-ní-zi a-tá* |("CAPERE₂")‖*u-pa-ha*	and I brought the trophies? inside.
§ 14	*a-wa/i pi-i-na-'* |REGIO-*ni-ia-ti* (FULGUR)*pi-ha-mi-sa* SUPER+*ra/i-'* |PES-*wa/i-i-ha*	and I came up glorified from those lands.
§ 15	|*za-zi-ha-wa/i-mi-i* (DOMUS.SUPER) *ha+ra/i-sà-tá-ni-zi pa-ti-i-*a* ("ANNUS") *u-si* |AEDIFICARE-*MI-ha*	These upper floors? I built myself in that year,
§ 16	*wa/i-mi-ta-*a* mi-i-na-*a* DOMINUS-*na-i-ni-i-na* (DEUS)*kar-hu-ha-si-na* (DEUS) *ku*+AVIS-*pa-si-ha* CRUS.CRUS(-)*ní-ia-sa-ha-na* |LITUUS+*na-ha*	And I saw the procession of my lord Karhuhas and Kubabas for myself,
§ 17	*wa/i-ma-tá-*a* |*za*‖-*ti-i* |("PODIUM") *hu-ma-ti* |(SOLIUM)*i-sà-nú-wa/i-ha*	and I seated them on this podium,
§ 18a	("*350")*á-sa-ha+ra/i-mi-sà-pa-wa/i-ma-za* |*za-'* DEUS-*ní-za* |CUM-*ni* ANNUS-*sa-li-za-sa* |("PANIS")*tú+ra/i-pi-sa*	and the sacrifice for them (shall be) this: with the gods annual bread,
§ 18b	(DEUS)CERVUS₂+*ra/i-hu-ha-ia* 1 BOS	for Karhuhas, an ox and

(ANIMAL)-*sa* OVIS-*sa-ha*   sheep,

§ 18c   (DEUS)*ku*+AVIS-*pa-pa* 1 BOS (ANIMAL)-*sa* 1 OVIS(ANIMAL)-*wa/i-sa-ha*   for Kubabas, an ox and a sheep,

§ 18d   (DEUS)*sa₅*+*ra/i-ku* OVIS-*wa/i-sa* ("*478") *ku-tú-pi-li-sa-ha*   for Sarkus, a sheep and a KUTUPILI,

§ 18e   1 OVIS(ANIMAL)*wa/i-sa* |VIR-*ti-ia-tà-za* DEUS-*ní-za* || one sheep for the male gods,

§ 18f   [1 OVIS(ANIMAL)*wa/i*]-*sa* [FEMINA-*ti*]-*ia*-[*ta*]-*za* [DEUS-*ni-za* ...]   [one she]ep for the fe[male gods, ...]

§ 19   [... REL]-*sa* *z*[*a-ti*]-*ia-za* [DEUS-*n*]*i*?-*za* MALUS-*ta₄-ti-i-*' || VERSUS-*ia-ni* |PES-*wa/i-ti*   [... wh]o(?) comes towards these [gods] with badness,

§ 20 |NEG₂-*pa-wa/i-sa* |*za-ti-ia-za* (DOMUS.SUPER)*ha*+*ra/i-sà-tá-na-za* MALUS-*ta₄-ti-i-*' |VERSUS-*ia-ni* [PES]-*wa/i-ti*   or comes towards these upper floors? with badness,

§ 21   [|]NEG₂-[*pa*]-*wa/i-tà* CRUS.CRUS[(-)*ni*?]-*ia-za-i* REL-*a-ti* PRAE-*na*   or if it shall pass down to (someone),

§ 22   [*wa/i*]-*tà*-*a [SCRIBA+*RA/I*](-)*tà*-[*i*] [|]REL-*i-sa*   who takes them/it ...

§ 23 |*za-a-zi-pa-wa/i-tá* [(SCALPRUM)] *ku-ta-sa₅*+*ra/i-zi-i* LOCUS-*ta₄-za* [(SA₄)*sá-n*]*í*||-*i-t*[*i*]   and [overthr]ows these orthostats in their places

§ 24 |NEG₂-pa-wa/i-tá |za-a-ti-ia-za |("SCALPRUM")ku-ta-sa₅+ra/i-za |á-ma-za |á-ta₅-ma-za |ARHA |"MALLEUS"-la/i/u-i

or erases my name on these orthostats,

§ 25 pa-ti-pa-wa/i-tá-*a CAELUM (DEUS) TONITRUS-sa (DEUS)kar-hu-ha-sá (DEUS) ku+AVIS-pa-pa-sá-ha (MONS)a+ra/i-pu-tá-wa/i-ni-sá-ha (DEUS)TONITRUS-sa ("FLUMEN+MINUS")sà-ku+ra/i-wa/i-ni-i-zi-ha (FLUMEN.REGIO)ha||-pa-tà-si DEUS-ní-zi |LIS-la/i/u-sa-tú

against him let the celestial Tarhunzas, Karhuhas and Kubabas, the Storm-God of the Arputaean mountain and the Sakuraean gods of the river-land litigate!

§ 26 wa/i-tú-*a |VIR-ti-ia-ti-ia-za-ha |("CULTER") pa+ra/i-tú-ní-tú-u

Let them sever? his masculinity,

§ 27 FEMINA-ti-ia-ti-ia-za-ha-wa/i-tú-u |("CULTER")pa+ra/i-tú-ni-i-tú

let them sever? her femininity,

§ 28 wa/i-tú-*a |VIR-ti-ia-ti-i-na |(*462)mu-wa/i-i-tà-na NEG₃-sa |tà-ti-i

and they shall not take to him male seed,

§ 29 FEMINA-ti-i[a]-ti-pa-wa/i-tú (FEMINA.*462) ||4?-tà |ni-i |tà-ti-i

(or) take to her female seed!

5.10   BABYLON 1

This stele from Babylon shows a Storm-God figure on its flat front and a seven-line inscription on its curved back which is well preserved but for a little damage. It was erected by an otherwise unattested prince-ruler who states that he dedicates his daughter and (a regular donation from?) all his possessions to the Storm-God of Aleppo as a thank-offering. The exact nature of the divine favour that he is repaying is not specified.

One may expect that the stele had originally been set up in the deity's temple at Aleppo and only later came to Babylon, presumably as booty. Dedication and monument, as customary, are protected by a protective curse. In contrast to many other such curses, it looks as if the author of this stele invokes the god not to punish potential offenders after the deed but to prevent it happening in the first place.

The style of the sculpture resembles the Suhis-Katuwas style of Karkamiš, c. 900 BC, thus providing an approximate date for the inscription. Note the use of both monumental and cursive sign forms, and especially the unusual shape of the hieroglyph *214 *ni* which lacks its top horizontal stroke.

📖 *Edition*: Hawkins, 2000, 391–394.

§§ 1–3:

"I (am) Laparizitis(?), the prince-ruler
For me the Halabean storm-god ran with favour
(and) to him I gave my dear daughter Anasis as a child"

§ 1   EGO-*wa/i-mi-i*   ¹*la*-PRAE-VIR?/*la*?-*sa* |("IUDEX")*tara/iwa/i-ní-sa*
      amu = wa = mi   *Lapariziti*(?) = *s*   *tarwani = s*
      I (am) qpt. refl.   **Laparizitis(?)** n.sg.C   **the ruler(?)** n.sg.C

|CAPUT-*ti-i-sa*   § 2   *wa/i-mu-ta-*a*   TONITRUS.*HALPA-pa-wa/i*ⁱ-*ní-sa*
      = *s*   *a = wa = mu = ta*   *halpa = wan = i = s*
the prince n.sg.C   **and** qpt. **for me** lpt.   **Halabean** eth. mut. n.sg.C

|| (DEUS)TONITRUS-*sa* |BONUS-*ti-i* |HWI-*ia-ta*
tarhunza = s   *wasara = ati*   *hwiya = ta*
Tarhunzas n.sg.C   **with favour** abl.   **he ran** 3.sg.prt.

§ 3   *wa/i-tu-*a*   *mi-i-na-*a*   ¹FEMINA-*ti-i-na* |BONUS-*mi-i-na*
      a = wa = tu   *am(a) = i = n*   *wanati = n*   = *m = i = n*
      and qpt. **to him**   **my**   mut. a.sg.C   **female** a.sg.C   **dear** mut. a.sg.C

|INFANS-*ní-i-na*   ¹*á-na-si-na* || *pi-ia-ha*
      niwaran(a) = i = n   *anasi = n*   *piya = ha*
(as a) child   mut. a.sg.C   **Anasis** a.sg.C   **I gave** 1.sg.prt.

---

¹*la*-PRAE-VIR?/*la*?, 'Laparizitis(?)- [PN]   INFANS-*na/i*-, 'child'
(IUDEX)*tarwani*- CAPUT-*ti*-, 'prince-ruler(?)'   *Anasi*-, 'Anasis' [PN]

☞ Both *la* signs in ¹*la*-PRAE-VIR?/*la*?-*sa* have added, unexplained strokes.
☞ ¹FEMINA: the personal marker may indicate a personal name 'Lady'.
☞ *Anasis* could also be a possessive adjective 'of Ana/is'.

§§ 4–6:

"All that (is) mine
whether it (be) the border of a (piece of) land
or the border of a vineyard

§ 4 |á-ma-za-pa-wa/i-'   REL-a-za |ta-ní-ma-za
      ama = n = za = pa = wa   kwa = n = za   tanima = n = za
      my a.sg.N npt. cpt. qpt.   **that** a.sg.N npt.   **all**   a.sg.N npt.

§ 5 |ma-wa/i-sa |"TERRA"-si |"FINES"-sa
      man = wa = as   *taskwira = asi   irha = s
      whether qpt. **it**   **of the land** g.sg.   **the border**   n.sg.C

§ 6 |ma-pa-wa/i-sa |"VITIS"-si-i |"FINES"-sa
      man = pa = wa = as   tuwarsa = asi   irha = s
      or   cpt. qpt. **it**   **of a vineyard** g.sg.   **the border**   n.sg.C

---

tanima/i-, 'all'   TERRA = *taskwira/i-*, 'land'
man ... man, 'whether ... or'   VITIS = *tuwarsa-*, 'vineyard'

☞ The form *kwanza* (REL-*a-za*) could be either nominative or accusative; here
   it must be the latter because it is the object to *pari piyaha* in § 9.
☞ Note that *-as* is common gender, agreeing with *irhas*; but we translate 'it'
   because in English we do not refer to the border as 'he/she'.

§§ 7–9

or the border of a building
(that) which comes from somewhere
before him, the Halabean Storm-God, I handed it over"

§ 7 |ma-pa||-wa/i-sa |"AEDIFICIUM"-si-i |"FINES"-sa
     man = pa = wa = as   = asi   irha = s
     or   cpt.   qpt.   **it**   **of a building**   g.sg.   **the border**   n.sg.C

§ 8 REL-a-za   REL-i-ta   PES-i
             kwa = n = za   kwita   awi = i
     (that) which   a.sg.N npt.   **wherever (from)** **it comes** 3.sg.prs.

§ 9 wa/i-tu-tà-*a   TONITRUS.HALPA-pa-wa/i-ní
     a = wa = tu = ata   halpa = wan = i
     and qpt. **him** **it**   **Halabean** eth. d.sg.

(DEUS)TONITRUS-ti-i |pa+ra/i-na-' |PRAE-i   pi-ia-ha
          tarhunt = i   paran   pari   piya = ha
for the Storm-God d.sg. **before** postpos.   **I handed over** 1.sg.prt.

AEDIFICIUM, 'building'

☞ § 9: *tu* 'him' and the following datives are governed by the postposition *paran*.

☞ *-ata,* the object to *pari piyaha* takes up *kwanza* of § 4, summing up everything mentioned in the previous clauses.

§§ 10–12:

"Who comes inside, eats (and) drinks,
whether he (be) an inner? enemy
or an outer? enemy

§ 10 |a-tá-pa-wa/i-ta   REL-i-sa || |CRUS-i |(„*471")á-za-i
        anta = pa = wa = ta kwi = s   = i   aza = i
      inside cpt. qpt. lpt. **who** n.sg.C **he comes** 3.sg.prs. **he eats** 3.sg.prs.

pa-za-i
  paza = i
he drinks 3.sg.prs.

§ 11 |ma-pa-wa/i-sa   a-tá-ti-li-i-sa |ta/i₄-la/i/u-ní-sa-*a
        man = pa = wa = as   antatil = i = s   atalun(a) = i = s
      whether cpt. qpt. **he** **inner?** mut. n.sg.C   **enemy** mut. n.sg.C

§ 12 |ma-pa-wa/i-sa |ARHA-ti-i-li-sa |ta/i₄-la/i/u-ní-sa-*a
        man = pa = wa = as   arhatil = i = s   atalun(a) = i = s
      or   cpt. qpt. **he** **outer?** mut. n.sg.C   **enemy** mut. n.sg.C

CRUS, 'to come'   *antatil(i)-*, 'inner?'
anta CRUS 'to come inside'   *ataluna/i-*, 'enemy'
(*471)*aza-*, 'to eat'   *arhatil(i)*, 'outer?'
paza-, 'to drink'

☞ The verbs for eating and drinking both have the iterative suffix *-za*.
☞ For *ataluna/i-* cf. also Rieken–Yakubovich 2010: 204–205.

§§ 13–14

or this stele overthrows from its place
or he erases it"

§ 13	za-pa||-wa/i-ta					|(„"STELE")wa/i-ní-za	
	za	= ∅	= pa	= wa	= ta	wani(t) = ∅	= za
	this	a.sg.N	cpt.	qpt.	lpt.	**stele**	a.sg.N npt.

|"LOCUS"-ta₅-za-'			|(SA₄)sá-ni-ti-i	
*pita	= ant	= anza	sani	= ti
in its places	suff.	d.pl.	**he overthrows**	3.sg.prs.

§ 14	|NEG₂-pa-wa/i-tà	|ARHA	|MALLEUS-i	
	napa = wa = ata	arha		= i
	or qpt. **it**		**he erases**	3.sg.prs.

☞ *wani(t)-*: for the deletion of final dentals, cf. 2.4.

☞ These clauses, very common phrases of protective curses, are closely parallel to §§ 23-24 of the previous inscription. If you compare the two, you will see that *-ata* 'it' of § 14 takes up *ataman* 'the name' which is not expressed in this but in the previous text.

§ 15:

"may the Halabean Storm-God not give him ARA PATA to destroy!"

§ 15   [|pa]-ti-⌈pa⌉-wa/i-*a   TONITRUS.HALPA-pa-wa/i-ni-sa
       apat = i = pa = wa   halpa = wan = i = s
       him d.sg. cpt. qpt.   **Halabean** eth. mut. n.sg.C

(DEUS)TONITRUS-sa |ara/i-' |pa-ta |NEG₃-sa |pi-ia-i ||
   tarhunza = s   ara   pata   nis   piya = i
Tarhunzas n.sg.C   a.sg.N(?) a.sg.N(?) **may he not give** 3.sg.prs.

ARHA |DELERE-nu-u-na
arha   = una
       to destroy   inf.

---

ara- pata-, '?'

☞ Remember that a negative command uses the present indicative not the imperative; cf. 4.7.3.

☞ ara pata, two unknown words, appear to be the object to 'may he not give'. The meaning of this clause seems to be that the god is invoked to prevent the destruction by a potential offender rather than punish him after the event, as many other curses stipulate. Since Hittite has a word ara- 'right', could ara pata possible mean something along the lines of 'right (and) opportunity'?

✍ Read the entire text and check whether you have understood it.

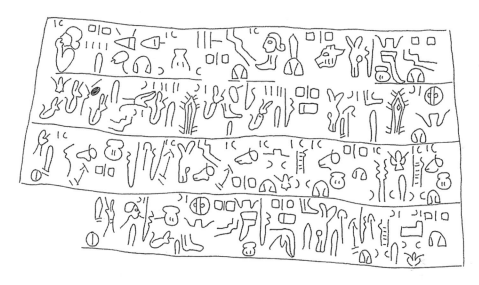

1 § 1   EGO-*wa/i-mi-i* ¹*la*-PRAE-VIR?/*la*?-*sa*   „I (am) Laparizitis(?),
        |("IUDEX")*tara/i-wa/i-ní-sa* |CAPUT-*ti-i-*   the prince-ruler,
        sa

2 § 2   *wa/i-mu-ta-**a TONITRUS.*HALPA-pa-*   For me the Halabean
        wa/i'-*ní-sa* ||(DEUS)TONITRUS-*sa*   Storm-God ran with
        |BONUS-*ti-i* |HWI-*ia-ta*   favour

   § 3   *wa/i-tu-***a mi-i-na-**a ¹FEMINA-*ti-i-na*   (and) to him I gave my
        |BONUS-*mi-i-na* |INFANS-*ní-i-na* ¹*á-na-*   dear daughter Anasis as
3   *si-na*|| *pi-ia-ha*   a child.

   § 4 |*á-ma-za-pa-wa/i-*' REL-*a-za* |*ta-ní-ma-za*   All that (is) mine

   § 5 |*ma-wa/i-sa* |"TERRA"-*si* |"FINES"-*sa*   whether it (be) the
                                                          border of a (piece of)
                                                          land

   § 6 |*ma-pa-wa/i-sa* |"VITIS"-*si-i* |"FINES"-*sa*   or the border of a
                                                          vineyard

4 § 7 |*ma-pa*||-*wa/i-sa* |"AEDIFICIUM"-*si-i*   or the border of a
        |"FINES"-*sa*   building

   § 8   REL-*a-za* REL-*i-ta* PES-*i*   (that) which comes from
                                                          somewhere

   § 9   *wa/i-tu-tà-**a TONITRUS.*HALPA-pa-wa/i-*   before him, the
        ní (DEUS)TONITRUS-*ti-i* |*pa+ra/i-na-*'   Halabean Storm-God, I
        |PRAE-*i pi-ia-ha*   handed it over.

5	§ 10	|a-tá-pa-wa/i-ta REL-i-sa|| |CRUS-i |(""*471")á-za-i pa-za-i	Who comes inside, eats (and) drinks,
	§ 11	|ma-pa-wa/i-sa a-tá-ti-li-i-sa |ta₄-la/i/u-ní-sa-'	whether he (be) an inner? enemy
	§ 12	|ma-pa-wa/i-sa |ARHA-ti-i-li-sa |ta₄-la/i/u-ní-sa-'	or an outer? enemy
6	§ 13	za-pa||-wa/i-ta |(„"STELE")wa/i-ní-za |"LOCUS"-ta₅-za-' |(SA₄)sá-ni-ti-i	or overthrows this stele from its place
	§ 14	|NEG₂-pa-wa/i-tà |ARHA |MALLEUS-i	or erases it
	§ 15	[|pa]-ti-⌈pa⌉-wa/i-*a TONITRUS.HALPA-pa-wa/i-ni-sa (DEUS)TONITRUS-sa	may the Halabean Storm-God not give him
7		|ara/i-' |pa-ta |NEG₃-sa |pi-ia-i || ARHA |DELERE-nu-u-na	ARA PATA to destroy!"

5.11   KULULU 4

The excerpts as shown above come from a funerary stele from Kululu, a rare example of a posthumous royal inscription. The text is written as a first person narrative, its author ostensibly the deceased Tabalean ruler Ruwas who reviews his life and lists the good deeds he committed. If Ruwas is correctly identified with the author of another inscription from Kululu (KULULU 1), namely 'Ruwas, servant of Tuwatis', the stele would be datable to Tuwatis reign or shortly thereafter, c. 750–740 BC.

A small separate inscription on top of the four-sided stele informs us who commissioned the monument: Hulis, a nephew of the ruler Ruwas. Since the stele is only half a metre high, this inscription too would have been easily visible.

The text contains only few word-dividers and among the mainly cursive sign forms one can note a surprisingly frequent use of two less common variants of the *sa*-series, sa_8 (*380) and sa_4 (*402). The former hieroglyph, a single vertical stroke (log. UNUS) may derive its phonetic value acrophonically from the Luwian word for 'one' which we would reconstruct as **sani*-.[39] Could sa_4 (log. SCUTELLA) possibly depict a seal impression and have derived its value acrophonically from *sasant*- 'sealed'?[40]

📖 *Edition*: Hawkins, 2000, 445–447.

---

39 Suggested by Neumann (pers. comm.).
40 Suggested by Nowicki (pers. comm.).

§§ 1–4:

"I was the ruler Ruwas, the Sun-God's offspring,
also my posterity(?) (is) the Sun-God's offspring
the gods loved my times
and they put into me a beloved soul."

§ 1   EGO-*wa/i-mi*   *ru-wa/i-sa₄*   IUDEX-*ní-sa*   *á-sa-ha*
       amu = *wa* = *mi*   *ruwa* = *s*   *tarwani* = *s*   *as* = *ha*
       I   qpt. refl.   **Ruwas** n.sg.C   **the ruler(?)** n.sg.C   **I was** 1.sg.prt.

SOL-*wa/i+ra/i-mi-sa₈*   § 2   NEPOS-*ta-ha-wa/i-mu*   SOL-*wa/i+ra/i-mi-sa₈*
   tiwarimi = *s*   = *ha* = *wa* = *mu*   *tiwarimi* = *s*
Sun-God's n.sg.C   **posterity(?) and** qpt. **for me**   **Sun-God's** n.sg.C
offspring   **offspring**

§ 3   AQUILA-*wa/i-mu*   DEUS-*ni-i-zí*   (LITUUS)*á-za-ta*
       ara = *wa* = *mu*   *masan(a)* = *i* = *nzi*   *aza* = *nta*
       times qpt. **for me** **the gods**   mut. n.pl.C   **they loved** 3.pl.prt.

§ 4   *wa/i-mu-ta* (LITUUS)*á-za-mi-na*   COR-*tara/i-na*   *a-ta*   *tu-tá*
       (a) =*wa*=*mu*=*ta*   *aza* = *(a)m(a)* = *i* = *n*   *atr(a)* = *i* = *n*   *anta*   *tu* = *nta*
       qpt. **me** lpt. **and**   **beloved** part. mut. a.sg.C   **soul** mut. a.sg.C **inside they put** 3.pl.prt.

Ruwa-, 'Ruwas' [PN]   AQUILA = *ara-*, 'time'
(SOL)*tiwarimi-*, 'offspring of the Sun-God'   COR = *atra/i-*, 'soul'
NEPOS-*ta*, 'posterity(?)'   *tu-*, 'to put'

☞ The past tense of the first clause identifies this text as a posthumous rather
   than a contemporary inscription.
☞ The common genealogical title *tiwatami-* (here rhotacised) can be analysed
   as compound noun *tiwat(a)-* 'Sun-God' plus an Anatolian suffix expressing
   family relationship *-mi(ya)* 'offspring of'.[41]

---

41 Cf. Neumann, 1996, 10.

§§ 6–8:

"And I was dear? to my lords
and they made me governor(?)
and I was house-lord in the lord's house."

§ 6   *wa/i-ta*   DOMINUS-*na-za-'*   *á-mi-ia-za*   BONUS-*si-ia-za-ha*
       (a) = wa = ta   *= anza*   *amiya = anza*   *= ha*
       and qpt. lpt. **to the lords** d.pl.   **my**   d.pl. **I was dear**? 1.sg.prt.

§ 7 |*wa/i-mu*   LEPUS+*ra/i-ia-la-ta*
       (a) = wa = mu   *tapariyala = nta*
       and qpt. **me**   **they made governor** 3.pl.prt.

§ 8   DOMINUS-*ni-ha-wa/i-mu*   DOMUS-*ní-i*
              = i = ha = wa = mu   *parn(a) = i*
       in the lordly d.sg. **and**   qpt. **for me** **in the house** d.sg.

DOMUS-*ni(-)*DOMINUS-*ni-i-sa₄*   *á-sá-ha*
                    = s   *as = ha*
            house-lord   n.sg.C   **I was**   1.sg.prt.

DOMINUS, 'lord'   DOMUS = *parna(n)-*, 'house'
BONUS-*si-ia-za-*, 'be dear to?'   DOMUS-*ni(-)*DOMINUS-*ni*, 'house-lord'
tapariyala-, 'make governor(?)'

☞ The compound noun DOMUS-*ni(-)*DOMINUS-*ni-i-sa₄* 'house-lord' appears
   to be the title of a prestigous office.

§§ 10–12

"And I blessed my lords well
and I was every man's father
and I honoured the good for every man."

§ 10 |wa/i-ta   á-mi-zi-i   DOMINUS-ni-zi |wa/i-su
        (a) = wa = ata   am(a) = i = nzi   = nzi   wasu
        and qpt. **them** **my**   mut. n.pl.C **lords** n.pl.C **well** adv.

u-sa₄-nú-wa/i-ha   § 11   OMNIS-ma-si-sa₄-ha-wa/i-mi
   usa = nuwa = ha   tanima = as(a) = i = s = ha = wa = mi
I blessed caus. 1.sg.prt.   **of every (man)**   p.adj. mut. n.sg.C **and** qpt. refl.

tá-ti-sa₄   á-sa₈-ha   § 12   a-wa/i   OMNIS-mi
   tat(a) = i = s   as = ha   (a) = wa   tanim(a) = i
father mut. n.sg.C **I was** 1.sg.prt.   **and** qpt.   **for every (man)**   d.sg.

sa-na-wa/i-sa₈   CUM-ní   i-zi-i-sa-ta-ha
   sanawi = ∅ = sa   izist = ha
the good a.sg.N npt.   prev.   **I honoured** 1.sg.prt.

---

wasu, 'well'   sanawi-, 'good'
usanuwa-, 'to bless'

☞ Unlike present forms, the past tense of the verb *as-* 'to be' tends to be
    written.

§ 15:

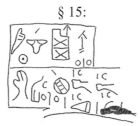

"This stele placed Hulis, Ruwas's brother's child."

§ 15 |*za-wa/i*   STELE   ᴵ*hu-li-sa₄* ||
        za = ∅ = *wa*   *wani(t)* = ∅ = *za*   *huli* = *s*
        this a.sg.N qpt.   **stele**   a.sg.N npt.   **Hulis**   n.sg.C

PONERE-*ta*   ᴵ*ru-wa/i-sa₈* |FRATER-*la-sa₈* |INFANS-*ni-sa₈*
    tuwa = *ta*   *ruwa* = *as*   **atala(?)* = *as*   = *s*
he placed 3.sg.prt.   **of Ruwas** g.sg. **of the brother** g.sg. **the child** n.sg.C

FRATER-*la* = **atala-(?)*, 'brother'   *huli*-, 'Hulis' [PN]

☞ Remember that the transcription *wani(t)*- for STELE is only a suggestion, cf. KARKAMIŠ A4b, §6.

Read the entire text and check whether you have understood it.

§ 1	EGO-*wa/i-mi ru-wa/i-sa₄* IUDEX-*ni-sa á-sa-ha* SOL-*wa/i+ra/i-mi-sa₈*	I was the ruler Ruwas, the Sun-God's offspring
§ 2	NEPOS-*ta-ha-wa/i-mu* SOL-*wa/i+ra/i-mi-sa₈*	and my posterity (is) the Sun-God's offspring
§ 3	AQUILA-*wa/i-mu* DEUS-*ni-i-zi* (LITUUS)*á-za-ta*	the gods loved my times,
§ 4	*wa/i-mu-ta* (LITUUS)*á-za-mi-na* COR-*tara/i-na a-ta tu-tá*	and they put into me a beloved soul.
§ 6	*wa/i-ta* DOMINUS-*na-za-' á-mi-ia-za* BONUS-*si-ia-za-ha*	And I was dear? to my lords,
§ 7	|*wa/i-mu* LEPUS+*ra/i-ia-la-ta*	and they made me governor(?),
§ 8	DOMINUS-*ni-ha-wa/i-mu* DOMUS-*ní-i* DOMUS-*ni(-)*DOMINUS-*ni-i-sa₄ á-sá-ha*	and I was house-lord in the lord's house.
§ 10	|*wa/i-ta á-mi-zi-i* DOMINUS-*ni-zi* |*wa/i-su u-sa₄-nú-wa/i-ha*	And I blessed my lords well,
§ 11	OMNIS-*ma-si-sa₄-ha-wa/i-mi tá-ti-sa₄ á-sa₈-ha*	and I was every man's father,
§ 12	*a-wa/i* OMNIS-*mi sa-na-wa/i-sa₈* CUM-*ní i-zi-i-sa-ta-ha*	and I honoured the good for every man.

| § 15 | \|*za-wa/i* STELE ¹*hu-li-sa₄* \|\| PONERE-*ta* ¹*ru-wa/i-sa₈* \|FRATER-*la-sa₈* \|INFANS-*ni-sa₈* | This stele Hulis, Ruwas's brother's child, placed. |

5.12   ASSUR letters

On 12.7.1905, the excavations at Assur unearthed seven thin lead strips with Hieroglyphic writing, rolled up and buried together with an Old-Assyrian cuneiform tablet under the floor of a house. One assumes that the owner of the house interred these objects for their alleged magical properties. We know that lead was used as a writing material also in Kululu - economic documents in Hieroglyphic Luwian survive - and amongst other ancient peoples such as the Egyptians and Phoenicians. Lead, a by-product of silver mining and readily available in Anatolia, is a very pliable metal and can easily be impressed even with a finger nail. In contrast to the more frequent stone inscriptions which were crafted by a mason, the lead documents from Assur and Kululu are in fact the only surviving examples of hieroglyphic handwriting.

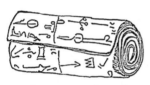

letter *e*, as found

As in the case of the objects from Babylon, Assur is an unlikely provenance, one assumes the letters would have come there as booty. Internal evidence from the letters suggests Karkamiš as the place of origin. On epigraphic criteria the letters are dated late, namely to the 8th century BC.

The letters are correspondence between businessmen, containing demands for merchandise and reproaches for not sending it. Only two lead strips (*e* and *f*) of the excavated letters survive today, some excerpts from them are presented in the following. Naturally, one would not expect to find the same kind of normative literary language employed for royal inscriptions in personal correspondence, and indeed, the style and content differ from the stone inscriptions. An added difficulty is the lack of comparable material. Many words, and even some grammatical forms are without parallel and therefore difficult to understand. But the letters also contain much desired attestations of otherwise rare forms, such as verbal forms of the second person.

📖 *Edition*: Hawkins, 2000, 533–555.

e, §§ 1–3:

"Say to Pihamis, Haranawizas speaks:
Peace (be) with you!
You are fallingin error(?) as regards writing!"

§ 1 |*á-sa₅-za*   [[]*pi-ha-mi* |*hara/i-na-wa/i-za-sa-wa/i-'*
      asaza = Ø   *Pihami* = *i*   *Haranawiza* = *s* = *wa*
      Say   2.sg.imp. **to Pihamis** d.sg   **Haranawizas**   n.sg.C qpt.

("LOQUI"-')*ha-ri+i-ti*   § 2 [|]*sa-pi-su+ra/i-wa/i-a-ti*
      hari = *ti*   *sapisur* = Ø = *wa* = *ti*
he speaks   3.sg.prs.   **health**   n.sg.N qpt.   **to you**

§ 3 |*u-sa-ta(-)mu-ti-sà-ha-wa/i-'* |*ha-tu+ra/i-'*
          ustamu = *tis* = *ha* = *wa*   *hat* = *ur* = *a*
      you fall in error(?) 2.sg.prs. **and** qpt.   **for writing** v.noun d.sg.

---

asaza-, 'to say'   *hatura*-, 'letter'
(LOQUI)*hati-/hari*-, 'to speak'   *hat*-, 'to write'
pihami-, 'Pihamis' [PN]   *ustamu*-(?), 'fall in error(?)'
haranawiza-, 'Haranawizas' [PN]
sapisur-, 'health'

☞ The Assur letters frequently write space fillers smaller than the other hieroglyphs, see the name Haranawizas; compare also *e*, §§ 13-14.

☞ The verbal noun in -*ur* (here *sapisur*) supplies the cases of the infinitive, its forms appear to be neuter.

☞ The suggested analysis of an otherwise unexplained *ustamutis(a)* as 'falling in error, making a mistake' is based on parallel words occurring in Hittite and would make good sense in view of the following reproaches.[42]

---

42 Suggested by Neumann (pers.comm.).

e, §§ 4–6:

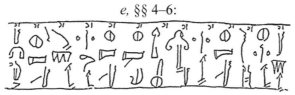

"(Are) we to write back ourselves?
We (are) to write no letter
You yourselves must write!"

§ 4 |a-za₅-za-ha-wa/i-za |á-pi |ha-tu-ra+a
    anzanz(a) = *ha* = *wa* = *anza*   *api*   *hat* = *ur* = *a*
    we n.pl.C **and** qpt. refl.   **back** **for writing** v.noun d.sg.

§ 5 |wa/i-za |NEG₂-' |REL-*i-ha* |ha-tu+ra/i-na
    (a) = *wa* = *anza*   *na kwi* = *n* = *ha*   *hatura* = *n*
    and qpt. **to us**   **none** a.sg.C indef.   **a letter** a.sg.C

|ha-tu-ra+a   § 6 |wa/i-ma-za |u-za₅-za
    hat = *ur* = *a*   *(a)* = *wa* = *manza*   *unzanz(a)*
for writing v.noun d.sg.   **and** qpt. **yourselves**   **you** n.pl.C

|ha-tu-ra+a |a-sa-ta-ni
    hat = *ur* = *a*   *as* = *tani*
for writing v.noun d.sg.   **you are** 2.pl.prs.

---

anzanz(a), 'we'   NEG₂ REL- -*ha* = *na kwa/i-* -*ha*, 'no one'
api, 'back'   -*manza*, 'yourselves'
REL-*i-ha* = *kwis-ha*, 'someone'   *unzanz(a)*, 'you'

☞ Note the rhetorical question of § 4.
☞ For *432, *za₅* and the spread of dative *anzanz(a)*, *unzanz(a)* to the nominative, s. Yakubovich 2010a: 79–83.
☞ The verb *as-* 'to be' with the dative expresses an obligation.

e, §§ 7–9:

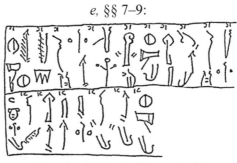

"Hear your kind of letter back!
Do we need to write back?
Or why did I make it, this letter of mine?"

§ 7 |a-wa/i |á-pi |u-zi-na |REL-i |ha-tu+ra/i-na
      a = wa   api   unz(a) = i = n   kwi   hatura = n
      and qpt. **back** **your** mut. a.sg.C indef.(?) **letter** a.sg.C

|AUDIRE+MI-ta-ra+a-nu § 8 |wa/i-za |á-pi |a-za₅-za-ha
*tuma(n)ti = ranu   (a) = wa = anza   api   anzanz(a) = ha
hear   2.pl.imp.   **and** qpt. **ourselves** **back** **we** n.pl.C **and**

|ha-tu+ra/i-' || § 9   ni-pa-wa/i-na |á-mu |REL-za
      hat = ur = a   nipa = wa = an   amu   kwanza
for writing v.noun d.sg.   **or** qpt. **it**   **I**   **why**

|i-zi-ia-wa/i |á-mi-na |za-na |ha-tu+ra/i-na
  iziya = wi   am(a) = i = n   za = n   hatura = n
I make 1.sg.prs. **my** mut. a.sg.C **this** a.sg.C **letter** a.sg.C

---

unza/i-, 'your'   REL-za = kwanza(?) 'why'

☞ In main clauses, REL(-*i*) is occasionally used as an indefinite particle.
☞ 1.pl.imp. -*ranu* rhotacised from -*tanu*.

e, §§ 12–14:

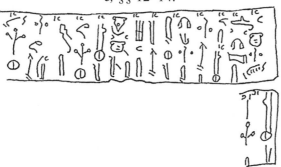

"And now let our lord's and our goods miss you in no way
and may they not let us go
nor cause me to die!"

§ 12 |u-nu-ha-wa/i-ma-za-ta |ní-i |ma-nu-ha
     unun = ha = wa = manza = ta   ni manuha
     now   and   qpt.   **you**   lpt.   **in no way**

|ARHA-ʾ ("COR")pa+ra/i-ra+a-ia |DOMINUS-ni-i |a-za-ia-ha-ʾ
 arha   para = ia   = i   anza = aya = ha
prev.   **let it miss** 3.sg.prs.   **the lordly** n.pl.N   **our**   n.pl.N   **and**

|sa-na-wa/i-ia   § 13 |wa/i-za⁻ⁱ |ní-i |ARHA
sanawi = a   (a) = wa = anza   ni   arha
goods   n.pl.N   **and** qpt. **us**   **not**   prev.

|("*69")sa-tu⁻ⁱ   § 14 |ni-pa-wa/i-mu || ARHA-ʾ |MORI-nu⁻ⁱ
 sa = ntu   nipa = wa = mu   arha   *walanu = ∅
let go 3.pl.imp.   **or**   qpt. **me**   **let die**   2.sg.imp.

---

ni manuha, 'in no way'   arha sa-, 'to leave, let go'
arha para-, 'to miss, lack'   arha MORI = *walanu-, 'to cause to die'
anza/i- 'our'

☞ § 12: Neuter plural subjects may take a singular verb, cf. 4.1.

☞ The writing sa-tu⁻ⁱ clearly identifies i as a space filler (note its small size in wa/i-za-ⁱ and in |MORI-nu⁻ⁱ); it cannot be part of the verbal ending -tu. Though less frequent than *450 a, the sign *209 i occurs as a space filler also in some other inscriptions, notably from Maraş.

f, §§ 11–13:

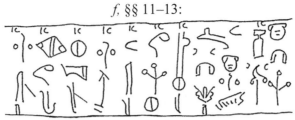

"Since you (are) to write
by no means abandon us,
nor cause me harm!"

§ 11 |*wa/i-ri+i*ⁱ |*ku-ma-na* |*ha-tu-ra+a*
       (a) = wa = ri   *kuman*   *hat = ur = a*
       and qpt. **you**   **since**   **for writing** v.noun d.sg.

§ 12 |*wa/i-za* |*ni-i-'* |*ma-nu-ha* |*ARHA-'* |("*69")*sa-si*ⁱ
       (a) = wa = anza   *ni manuha*   *arha   sa = si*
       and qpt.   **us**   **in no way**   prev. **let go** 2.sg.prs.

§ 13   *ni-pa-wa/i-mu*   ("SIGILLUM")*hwi/a-pa-sa-nu*
       nipa = wa = mu   *hwapasa = nu = ∅*
       or   qpt. **me**   **cause harm** caus. 2.sg.imp.

---

kuman, 'since'   (SIGILLUM)*hwapasanu-*, 'cause harm'

☞ *-ri* is the rhotacised form of the enclitic reflexive personal pronoun *-ti* 'you'.
☞ If you compare the last two clauses with the closely parallel §§ 13-14 on the
   previous page, you will notice that a negative command may be expressed
   with either the imperative (e, § 13) or the indicative present (f, § 12). The
   use of the indicative is the more usual construction, the imperative occurs
   only in few, late examples.

☝ Read the entire text and check whether you have understood it.

e, § 1	|*á-sa5-za* [|]*pi-ha-mi* |*hara/i-na-wa/i-za-sa-wa/i-'* ("LOQUI"-')*ha-ri+i-ti*	"Say to Pihamis, Haranawizas *speaks*:
§ 2	[|]*sa-pi-su+ra/i-wa/i-a-ti*	Peace (be) with you!
§ 3	|*u-sa-ta-mu-ti-sà-ha-wa/i-'* |*ha-tu+ra/i-'*	You are falling in error(?) as regards writing!
§ 4	|*a-za5-za-ha-wa/i-za* |*á-pi* |*ha-tu-ra+a*	(Are) we to write back ourselves?
§ 5	|*wa/i-za* |NEG2-' |REL-*i-ha* |*ha-tu+ra/i-na* |*ha-tu-ra+a*	We (are) to write no letter,
§ 6	|*wa/i-ma-za* |*u-za5-za* |*ha-tu-ra+a* |*a-sa-ta-ni*	you yourselves must write!
§ 7	|*a-wa/i* |*á-pi* |*u-zi-na* |REL-*i* |*ha-tu+ra/i-na* |AUDIRE+*MI-ta-ra+a-nu*	Hear your kind of letter back!
§ 8	|*wa/i-za* |*á-pi* |*a-za5-za-ha* |*ha-tu+ra/i-'* ||	Do we need to write back?
§ 9	*ni-pa-wa/i-na* |*á-mu* |REL-*za* |*i-zi-ia-wa/i* |*á-mi-na* |*za-na* |*ha-tu+ra/i-na*	Or why did I make it, this letter of mine?"

e, § 12 |*u-nu-ha-wa/i-ma-za-ta* |*ní-i* |*ma-nu-ha*   "And now let our lord's
           |*ARHA-*' ("COR")*pa+ra/i-ra+a-ia*   and our goods miss you
           |DOMINUS-*ni-i* |*a-za-ia-ha-*' |*sa-na-*   in no way,
           wa/i-ia

   § 13 |*wa/i-za^{-i}* |*ní-i* |ARHA |("*69")*sa-tu^{-i}*   and may they not let us
                                                               go,

   § 14 |*ni-pa-wa/i-mu* || ARHA-' |MORI-*nu^{-i}*   nor cause me to die!"

f, § 11 |*wa/i-ri+i^{-i}* |*ku-ma-na* |*ha-tu-ra+a*   "Since you (are) to write,
   § 12 |*wa/i-za* |*ni-i-*' |*ma-nu-ha* |ARHA-' |("*69")   by no means abandon us,
           sa-sī^{-i}

   § 13   *ni-pa-wa/i-mu* ("SIGILLUM")*hwi/a-pa-sa-*   nor cause me harm!"
           nu

a- [conj.], 'and'

a(ya)- [v.], 'to make'

ala/i/unama- [noun, C., det. COR], 'envy, covetousness'

ala/i/unaza- [v., det. COR], 'to covet, desire'

ama/i-, amiya- [poss.pron.], 'my'

amiya-, s. ama/i-

amu [pers.pron.], 'I'

-an [pers.pron.], 'him, her, it'

anan [prev./adv./postpos.+d., SUB-*na-na*], 'under'

anantara/i- [adj., INFRA-*tara/i-*], 'lower'

anat(i)- [noun, C.], 'mother'

anta [prev./postpos.+d.], 'in, inside'

antan [prev.], 'in, into'

antatil(i)- [adj.], 'internal, inner'

anza/i- [poss.pron.], 'our'

anzanz(a) [pers.pron.], 'we'

-anza [pers.pron.], 'we, us'

apa- [dem.pron.], 'that'

apan [conj., prev./postpos.+d., POST-*na/-ni*], 'behind, after; afterwards, in future'

apara/i- [adj., POST+*ra/i-*], 'later'

apari, s. apati

apati [adv.], 'there'

api [adv.], 'back'

apin [dem.pron., abl. of *apa-*], 'with/from that'

ar- [v., log. "PES$_2$"], 'to come'

araiy(a)- [adj., det./log. LONGUS], 'long'

ara/i- [noun, C.], 'age'

ara pata [noun, N.(?)], '?'

arawan(i)- [adj.], 'free'

arha [postpos.+abl./prev./adv.], 'forth, away; completely'

arhatil(i)- [adj.], 'outer'

arma- [noun, C.], 'moon; month'

arut(i)- [noun, C., log. "*78"], 'wing, basket(?)'

as- [v.], 'to be'; *anta as-* (+d.) 'to be inside'; *api as-*, 'to be behind, remain'

-as [encl.pers.pron.], 'he, she'

asa- [v., log. SOLIUM(+*MI*)], 'to sit; dwell'; *anta asa-*, 'to live in'

asa- [noun., C., log. MENSA.SOLIUM], 'seat'

asaza- [v.], 'to speak, proclaim'; *asazama/i-* [part.], 'declared, pronounced'

ashar- [noun, N.], 'blood'
asharmis(a)- [noun, N., log. *350], 'sacrifice?; blood-offering?'
-asa/i- [gen.adj.]
asu- [noun, C., det. SCALPRUM], 'stone'
-ata [pers.pron.], 'it; they, them'
at-/az- [v., log. EDERE], 'to eat'
atala- [noun, C., log. FRATER(?) / INFANS(.NI)], 'brother(?)'
ataluna/i- [noun, C.], 'enemy'
ataman- [noun, N.], 'name'
atanasma- [noun, log. "COR"], 'wisdom'
atani- [noun, C.], 'enemy'
atla/i-, s. *atra/i-*
atan(i)-, s. *atra/i-*
atra/i- [noun, C., log. COR], 'soul; person'
atu(i)- [noun, N., log. MALUS], 'evil'
atuwit- [noun, N., log. MALUS], 'evil, badness'
atuwari- / atuwati- [adj., log. MALUS], 'bad, evil'
awi- [v., log. "PES$_2$"], 'to come'; *apan(i)* (POST-*na/i*) *awi-*, 'to come after,
    become available'; *arha awi-*, 'to come forth'; *sara* (SUPER+*ra/i*) *awi-*, 'to
    come up'; *tawiyan* (VERSUS-*na*) *awi-*, 'to come towards, approach'; *wala
    awi-*, 'to come ill (for)'
az-, s. *at-*
aza- [v., det. LITUUS], 'to love'
azama/i- [v.part.] 'loved'
azali(ya)- [noun, N., det. PANIS.PITHOS], 'food, feast'
anzanz [pers.pron.], 'we'
azu(wa)- [noun, C., log. EQUUS.ANIMAL], 'horse'
azusantala- [v., log. "ANIMAL.EQUUS"], 'to ride'

-ha [cpt.], 'and; even, also'
hali(ya)- [noun, N., log. DIES], 'day'
hamsa/i- [noun, C., log. INFANS.NEPOS], 'grandson'
hamsukala- [noun, C., log. INFANS.NEPOS], 'great-grandson'
haniyatastra/i- [noun, N., log. MALUS$_{(2)}$], 'evil, badness'
haniyata(iya)- [noun, N. / adj., log. "MALUS$_2$"], 'evil'
*hantahit- [noun, N.], 'preeminence'
*hantawat(i)- [noun, C., log. REX], 'king'
*hantawatahi(t)- [noun, N., log. REX], 'kingdom, kingship'
hant(i)- [noun, N., log. FRONS], 'face';
hanti [adv., postpos.+d., FRONS-*ti*], 'against; in front of; before'
hanti(?) [postpos., PRAE-*ti*], 'before'
hanti(ya)- [adj., log. FRONS], 'former, first; special'

hantil(i)- [adj., log. FRONS], 'former, first; special'; *sarli hantili*- 'highly pre-eminent'

hapa/i- [noun, C., log. FLUMEN], 'river'

hapari-, s. hapata/i-

hapata/i- [noun, C., log. FLUMEN.REGIO], 'river-land'

hara-, s. hata-

hara/ila/i- [noun, C., log. SCUTUM], 'shield'

haranu-, [v.caus., log. LOQUI], 'to make speak'

hari-, s. hati-

haristana/i- [noun, C., log. DOMUS.SUPER], 'upper floors(?)'

harmaha/i- [noun, C., log. CAPUT], 'head'

harnisa(n)- [noun, N., log. CASTRUM], 'fortress'

harpa- [noun, C., log. *219], 'rebel(?)'

hartu- [noun, C., det. INFANS], 'descendant'

harwa- [noun, C., log. "VIA"], 'road'

harwani- [v., log. VIA], 'to send'

harwantahit- [noun, N., log. VIA], 'travelling'

has- [v.], 'to beget'

has- [noun, N., log. "*314]", 'bone'

LINGERE(-)*hasa*- [noun, C.], 'luxury(?)'

*hastala/i- [noun, C., log. HEROS], 'hero'

hasu- [noun, C., log. NEPOS], 'family'

hat- [v.], 'to write'

hata- [v.], 'to demolish(?), destroy'

hatal(a)i- [v., log. *274], 'to smite'

hatama- [adv. / noun, N.pl.?, det. *464], 'ruinously / ruin(?)'

hatara/i- [noun], 'life'

hatastra/i- [noun, N., log. *314], 'horror, violence'

hati- [v., log. LOQUI], 'to speak'

hatur- [v.noun, N.], 'writing'

hatura- [noun, C.], 'letter'

haturala- [noun], 'messenger'

hawa/i- [noun, C., log. OVIS], 'sheep'

hazi- [v.], 'to engrave'

haz(iy)ani- [noun, C., log. LIGNUM], 'mayor'

haziwit- [noun, N., log. *314 / LIGNUM], 'ritual'

hinu(wa)- [v.caus., log. "PES$_2$"], 'to cause to pass'

hirut- / *hirur*- [noun, N., log. "*476(.311)"], 'oath'

hishi- [v., log. PUGNUS.PUGNUS], 'to bind'

huha- [noun, C., log. AVUS], 'grandfather'

huhat(i)- [noun, C., log. AVUS], 'great-grandfather'

huhatala/i- [adj., log. AVUS], 'ancestral'

huhurpal(i)- [noun, N.?, log. "LIGNUM"], '(part of the) war chariot(?)'

humt(i)- [noun, C., log. PODIUM], 'podium'

hwapasa- [v., log. "SIGILLUM"], 'to harm'

hwapasanu- [v.caus., log. "SIGILLUM"], 'to cause harm'

hwi(ya)- [v., log. PES₂], 'to run'; *hwihwi(sa)-* [v.redupl.], 'to march'; PRAE-*na hwiya-* 'to run before'

hwisar-, s. *hwitar-*

hwitar- [noun, N., log. "ANIMAL.BESTIA"], 'wild animal'

i- [v., "PES₂"], 'to go'; *arha i-*, 'to go forth, die'; *tawiyan i-*, 'to go towards, approach'

iyari- [v., log. LONGUS], 'to extend'; *arha iyari-*, 'to extend'

i(ya)sa- [v.], 'to buy'

imani- [v., log. OCCIDENS], 'to destroy'

imatuwan(i)- [adj.], 'Hamathite'

ipama- [noun, N., log. OCCIDENS / SOL], 'west'

irha/i- [noun, C., log. "FINES"], 'border, frontier; area'

irhala/i- [noun, C.], 'frontier-post'

iri(ya)- [noun, N.], 'drawing, carving, portrait'

irwa- [noun, log. GAZELLA], 'gazelle'

isan(a)- [noun, plural form with singular meaning, log. "LECTUS"], 'bed'

isanu(wa)- [v.caus., log. SOLIUM(+MI)], 'to make sit; settle; cause to dwell'

istar(a)ta- / istar(a)la- [noun, N., log. THRONUS], 'throne, seat'

istra/i- [noun, C., log. MANUS], 'hand'

izi(ya)- [v.], 'to make'; *anan izi(ya)-*, 'to subject'; *saranta* (SUPER+*ra/i-ta*) *izi(ya)-* [+ Dat.], 'to make (one) upon (another), i.e. to increase, enlarge'

izista- [v.], 'to honour'

izistra/i- [noun, C./N.?], 'honour'

iziyana- [noun, C.], 'deed; ritual(?)'

iziyat(a)ra- [noun, N.], 'performance, ritual'

kaluna-, s. *karuna-*

*karmal- [noun, N., log. ASCIA], 'axe'

karmali- [v., log. ASCIA], 'to hack'; *arha karmali-*, 'to hack down'

karuna- [noun, C., log. "*255"], 'granary'

*kata [prev., log. INFRA(-*ta*)], 'down, below'

*katanta [adv., log. INFRA-*ta-ta*], 'down'

katina- [noun, N., log. "SCALPRUM"], 'bowls'

kistama/i- [noun, N., log. ORIENS], 'east'

*kumaiy(a)- [adj., log. PURUS], 'pure'

kuman [conj.], 'since, because; when; while'

kumani- [v., log. "PURUS"], 'to consecrate'

kumapi [postpos.+d.], 'together with(?)'

kumastra/i- [noun, C.], 'sacrament'

kumaza- [noun, C.], 'priest'

kutasara/i- [noun, C., det. SCALPRUM], 'orthostat'

kutasari- [v., log. SCALPRUM], 'to orthostate (to put up orthostats?)'

kutupili- [noun, C., det. *478], 'lamb(?) (an animal smaller than a sheep)'

*kuwalan- [noun, N., log. EXERCITUS], 'army'

kwa(n)za [conj., REL-*za*], 'since, because; why; even though'

kwaya- [v.], 'to fear'

kwari [conj., log. REL+*ra/i(-i)*, REL-*ri*+*i*], 'because, since; as, as if, like; if; when'

kwati [conj., log. REL*(-a)-ti*], 'if; (so) that; wherefore; when(?)'

kwaza- [v., log. CAPERE+SCALPRUM, REL-*za*-], 'to cut, engrave'

kwi [conj., REL-*i*], 'even though; when, while'

kwi [indef.pt.], 'kind of(?)'

kwi-/kwa- [rel.pron., REL], 'who, which'

kwis-ha [indef.pron., REL-*ha*], 'someone'

kwipa [adv., REL-*i*-*pa*], 'indeed, so'

kwita(n) [adv., REL-*i*-*ta*], 'where, wherever'

kwita(n) kwita(n) [adv.], 'wheresoever'

la(la)- [v., log. "CAPERE" / "*69"], 'to take'; *arha la-*, 'to take away (from)'

*lalant(i)- [noun, C., log. "LINGUA"], 'tongue, language'

lamni [adv.], 'at the moment'

lara-, s. lata-

laranu- [v.caus.], 'cause to prosper'

lata- [v], 'to prosper'

MANUS(-)*latara-* [v.], 'to extend(?)'

luslus- [v., log. "FLAMMAE(?)"], 'to burn'

luzala/i- [adj.], 'sacrificial'

malitima/i- [adj., log. "PANIS"], 'honey-sweet'

mamu(t)- [noun, C.], 'partner(?)'

man [adv.], 'much'

man ... man ... [disj.], 'whether ... or ...; be it that ... or that ...'

mana- [noun, C., log. SCALPRUM], 'mina'

*mana- [v., log. LITUUS+*na*-], 'to see'; *anta* LITUUS+*na*-, 'to behold'; *anan* (SUB-*na-na*) LITUUS+*na*-, 'to despise'

manuha [adv.], *s. ni manuha*

-*manza* [pers. pron.], 'for them'

marati- [noun, C., log. "LOQUI"], 'request, order'

masana/i- [noun, C., det. DEUS], 'god'

mashani- [v.], 'to make grow'
matu- [noun, N., log. VITIS], 'wine'
-mi [refl.pron.], 'myself'
miya(n)ti- [adj.], 'many'
mu, s. amu
-mu [pers.pron.], '(for) me'
musanuwa(n)t(i)- [part., log. "PANIS.SCUTELLA"], 'satisfying(?)'
muwa/i- [noun, C., log. *273], 'strength, courage'
muwa- [v., log. *273], 'to conquer'
muwatala/i- [adj.], 'mighty, potent'
muwita- [noun, C., log. (FEMINA.)*462], 'seed'

na(wa) [neg., log. NEG$_2$], 'not'
na kwihan / hwihan(?) [neg.+adv.], 'not at all'
nanasra/i- [noun, log. FEMINA], 'sister'
napa [disj.], 'or'
nawa- [noun, C., log. INFANS], 'great-great-grandson'
nawanawa- [noun, C., log. INFANS], 'great-great-great-grandson'
nawarala/i- [adj.], 'foreign'
ni(s) [neg., log. NEG$_3$], 'not' (prohibitive)
ni manuha [neg.+adv.], 'in no way'
(ni)niya- [v., log. CRUS.CRUS], 'to turn, follow'; *(ni)niyaza-* [v.], 'to pass(?)'
CRUS.CRUS(-)*niyasatala-* [noun, C.], 'successor'
CRUS.CRUS(-)*niyasha-* [noun, C.], 'procession'
nimuwiza-, niwiza-, niza- [noun, C., log. INFANS], 'son'
nipa [disj.], 'or'
niwarana/i- [noun, C.], 'helpless, child'
niwiza-, s. nimuwiza-
niza-, s. nimuwiza-
nuwa/i- [num.], 'nine/ninth(?)'

-pa [pt.], 'but, and, also'
pa- [v., log. "PES$_2$"], 'to go, live'
panuwa- [v.caus.], 'to make drink'
paran [postpos./prev., PRAE-*na/i*], 'before, in front of'
par(iy)a(n)ti(?) [postpos., PRAE-*ti*], 'before'
partuni- [v., det. CULTER], 'to sever(?)'
arha para- [prev.+v.], 'to miss, lack'
pari [postpos.+d./prev., PRAE], 'over; before, in front of'
parna- [noun, N., log. DOMUS], 'house'
parnawa- [v., log. (DOMUS.)CRUX], 'to serve'
kata pas(a)- [v., log. EDERE], 'to swallow up, gulp down'

paskwa- [v.], 'to forget, neglect'

pata/i- [noun, C., log. PES], 'foot'

pata, s. *ara pata*

paza- [v.iter.], 'to drink'

paza- [v.iter., log. PES$_2$], 'to walk; live'

pihama/i- [v.part., log. FULGUR], 'glorified'

pihas- [noun, N., log. FULGUR], 'lightning; victory'

*pita(nt)- [noun, N., log. LOCUS], 'place; precinct'

*pita(n)ta *pita(n)ta [adv., log. LOCUS-*tá* LOCUS-*tá*], 'everywhere'

pin, s. *apin*

pipasa- [v.it.], 'to keep giving' [iter. of *piya-*]

pitahaliya- [v., log. LOCUS], 'to *exile*(?)'

piya- [v., log. DARE], 'to give'; *pari piya-* (PRAE DARE), 'to hand over'

sara (SUPER+*ra/i*) *pu-* [v.], 'to write above(?)'

pupala/i- [v., log. "LOQUI"], 'to write, compose(?)'

ruwan [adv.], 'formerly'

sa- [v., log. "*69"], 'to let, allow'; *arha sa-* [prev.+v.], 'to leave, let go'

sa- [v.], 'to press, seal; shoot'(?)

saha- [v.], '*to cure*(?)'

salha(t)- [noun, N., log. "LIGNUM"], 'succession, greatness'

saman- [noun, N.], 'sealing; contract, agreement'

sanawa/i- / sanawaiy(a) [adj., log. BONUS], 'good'

sanawi [adv. log. BONUS], 'well'

sanawa/istra/i- [noun, N., log. "BONUS"], 'goodness'

sanawiya- [v.], 'to be good'

sanawit- [noun, N.], 'the good, goodness'

san(a)i- [v., log. SA$_4$], 'to overturn, overthrow'

sapisara-, s. *sapisata-*

sapisata-, sapisara- [noun], 'health'

sapisur- [v.noun, N.], 'health, peace'

sara [postpos.+d./prev./adv, SUPER+*ra/i*], 'on, above; over, up'; *sara kata*
   (SUPER+*ra/i* INFRA-*ta*), 'up (and) down'

sara(n)ta [postpos.+d., SUPER+*ra/i-ta*], 'upon'

sarku- [adj.], 'mighty (one)'

sarlata- [noun, N., det. LIBARE], 'libation, offer'

sarla/i- [v., log. LIBARE], 'to libate, offer'; *sasarla-* [v.redupl.], 'to offer'

sarli- [adj., log. SUPER+*ra/i*], 'upper'

sasa- [noun, C., log. ANIMAL.GAZELLA], 'gazelle'

sasaliya- [noun, N., log. *262], 'shooting'

sasan- [noun, N., log. (SCALPRUM.)SIGILLUM], 'seal'

sasarla-, s. sarli-

-si [refl.pron.]

sukala- [noun, C., log. "LIGNUM"], 'vizier'

sura/i- [noun, C., log. "CORNU+*RA/I*"], 'plenty; fullness'

suwa- [v., det. "MANUS"], 'to fill'

suwan(i)- [noun, C., log. CANIS], 'dog'

¹*ta-* [v., log. "CRUS"], 'to stand'; *ta-* + inf. 'to begin to do something'; *taza-* [v.it.]

²*ta-* [v.], 'to put, place'

³*ta-* / *la-* [v., log. CAPERE], 'to take'; *arha ta-* 'to take up, take away'

-ta [local pt.]

tama- [v., log. AEDIFICARE(+*MI*)], 'to build'; *anda* AEDIFICARE+*MI*, 'to block up(?)'

tamihit- [noun, N.], 'abundance'

tanata/i- [adj., log. "VACUUS"], 'empty, devastated'

tanata- [v., log. "VACUUS"], 'to waste'

tanima/i- [adj., log. OMNIS], 'all, every'

tanisa- [noun, N., log. STELE], 'stele'

tanit(i)- [noun, C., log. FEMINA.PURUS.INFANS], 'hierodule'

tanuwa- [v.caus., log. CRUS], 'to make stand, set up'

tapariya- [noun, C., log. LIGNUM, LEPUS], 'authority'

tapariya- [v., log. LIGNUM.CRUS(-)LEPUS], 'to govern, decree'

*taparita- [noun, log. LEPUS+*RA/I*], 'authority'

*taparahit- [noun, N.], 'authority'

*tapariyala/i- [noun, C., log. LEPUS], 'governor'

*tapariyala- [v., log. LEPUS], 'to be/make governor'

tarkasna- [noun, C., log. ASINUS], 'donkey'

tarkasni- [noun, C., log. ASINUS₂], 'mule'

tarpala/i- [noun, C.], 'substitute'

tarpari- [v., log. *218], 'to lack'

tarsa- [noun, C.], 'leaf(?)'

taru(t)- [noun, N., log. "STATUA", "LIGNUM"], 'wood; image, statue'

taruwi(ya)- [adj., log. "LIGNUM"], 'wooden'

tarwani- [noun, C., log. IUDEX], 'ruler; judge(?)'

tarwan(a)- [noun, C.?, log. IUSTITIA], 'justice'

tasa- [noun, N., log. *256], 'stele'

*taskwira/i- [noun, C., log. "TERRA(-REL)"], 'earth, land; ground, territory'

tata/i- [noun, C.], 'father'

tatala/i- [adj.], 'paternal'

tatariya- [v., log. "LOQUI"], 'to curse'

tatari(ya)ma/i- [v. part., log. "LOQUI"], 'accursed'

tati(ya) [adj.], 'paternal'

tawa/i- [noun, sg. C., pl. N., log. "LITUUS", "COR"], 'eye'

tawana/i- [noun, C., log. DOMUS+SCALA], 'apartment'

tawiyan [postpos., log. VERSUS], 'towards'

taza- [v.iter., log. CRUS], 'to keep standing'

-ti [refl.pron.], '(for) himself, herself'

-ti [refl.pron.], '(for) yourself (sg.)'

tipas- [noun, N., log. CAELUM], 'sky, heaven'

tiyari(ya)- [v., det. LITUUS], 'to watch, guard'

tiwatami(ya)-, tiwara/imi(ya)- [noun, C., det. SOL], 'offspring of the Sun-God'

-tu [pers.pron.], 'for him, her'

-tu [pers.pron.], '(for) you (sg.)'

tu(wa)-, s. *tuwa-*

*tuma(n)ti- [v., log. AUDIRE+*MI*], 'to hear'; *pari *tumatima/i-*, 'far famed'

tunikala-, tunikara- [noun, C., det. "(PANIS.)SCUTELLA"], 'baker(?)'

tunikara-, s. *tunikala-*

tup(a)i- [v., log. *273], 'to smite'; *anda tup(a)i-*, 'to incise'

turpa/i- [noun, C., det. PANIS], 'bread'

tuwa- [v., det. PONERE], 'put, place; establish'; *pari tuwa-*, 'to place before, dedicate to'; *anan tuwa-*, 'to place under'

tuwa/i- [poss.pron.], 'your (2.sg.)'

tuwarsa- [noun, log. VITIS], 'vineyard'

tuwatar(i)- [noun, C., det. FILIA], 'daughter'

tuwa/i- [num.], 'two'

uliya-, s. *waliya-*

unanu- [v.caus., log. LITUUS], 'to cause to know'

uni- [v., log. LITUUS], 'to know'

unun [conj.], 'now'

unzanz(a) [pers.pron.], 'you'

unza/i- [poss.pron.], 'your (2.pl.)'

upa- [v., log. "CAPERE(2)"], 'to bring'; *arha upa-* 'to bring forth'

upa- [v., log. "PES₂"], 'to dedicate'

upana/i- [noun, C., det. SCALPRUM.CAPERE₂], 'trophy(?)'

*ura/i- [adj., MAGNUS+*ra/i-*], 'great'

*uranuwa- [v.caus., log. MAGNUS], 'make great, promote'

usa- [v., log. PES], 'to bring'

usa/i- [noun, C., log. ANNUS], 'year'

usala/i- [adj., log. ANNUS], 'annual'

usala/i- [noun, C., log. "*217"], 'robber'

usaliza- [adj.], 'annual'

usanuwa- [v.], 'to bless'; *arha usanuwama/i-* 'highly blessed'

usinasi-, s. wasinasi-
ustamu- [n.(?)], 'fall in error, make a mistake(?)'
*utni- [noun, N., log. REGIO], 'land'
u- [v., det. BIBERE], 'trinken'

-wa [qpt.]
wala-, wara- [v., log. MORI], 'to be ill, suffer'; *arha wala-*, 'to die'; **walanu-*
[v.caus.], 'to cause to die'
wala [adv., log. CRUX], 'ill; fatally'
waliya- [v., log. BONUS], 'to raise, exalt'; *apani anda waliya-* 'to exalt'
walilita-, walirita- [n., log. TERRA+LA+LA], 'field; plain'
*wanat(i)- [noun, C., log. FEMINA], 'woman'
*wanatiyant(i)- [adj.], 'female'
*wanatiyantiya- [noun, N.], 'femininity'
-wan(i)- [eth.suff.]
wani(t)- [noun, N., log. STELE], 'stone, stele'
wara-, *s. wala-* [v.]
warala/i- [adj.], 'own, proper'
wara/izani- [noun, C., log. CURRUS], 'chariot(ry)'
wariya- [noun, C.], 'help, assistance'
wariya- [v.], 'to help'
wariyamala [adv., log. BONUS], 'peacefully'
warpa/i- [noun, C., log. *273], 'courage, virtue, skill'
warpala/i- [adj., log. "SCALPRUM+*RA/I.LA/I/U*"], 'brave'
wasa- [v., log. "BONUS"], 'to be good, dear'
wasama/i- [v.part.], 'beloved'
wasar(a)- [noun, N.?, log. BONUS], 'favour, goodness'
wasi(ya)- [noun, N., log. MENSA], 'table'
wasinasa/i- [noun, C., log. *474], 'eunuch'
wasu [adv.], 'well'
wasu- [v., log. BONUS], 'to be good'
wawa/i- [noun, C., log. BOS], 'ox'
wazi- [noun, C., log. *69], 'request'
wiyan(a)- [noun, C., log. "VITIS"], 'vine'

za- [dem.pron.], 'this'
-za [npt.]
zahanu(wa)- [v.caus.], 'to make *attack*'
zalal(a)- [noun, N., log. *91/92/93], 'cart'
zan apan-ha [adv.], 'now and then(?)'
zari, *s. zati*
zarti- [v.], 'to desire, wish'

zar(t)- [noun, N., log. "COR"], 'heart; person, body'
zati [adv.], 'here'
zin... zin [adv.], 'on the one hand ... on the other'
*zita/i- [noun, C.], 'man'
*zitiyant(i)- [adj.], 'male'
*zitiyantiya- [noun, N.], 'masculinity'

Logograms

ADORARE [v.], 'to pray'
AEDIFICARE+*MI* [v., *tama*-]*,* 'to build'; *anda* AEDIFICARE+*MI*, 'to block up(?)'
"AEDIFICIUM" [noun], 'building'
AMPLECTI-*ma/i*- [v.part.], 'beloved (embraced)'
AMPLECTI-*nu*- [v.caus.], 'to cause to embrace'
ANIMAL.BESTIA [noun, N., *hwisar*-, *hwitar*-], 'wild animal'
ANNUS [noun, C., *usa/i*-], 'year'; [adj., *usala/i*-], 'annual'
AQUILA [noun, C., *ara/i*(?)], 'time(?)'
ARGENTUM [noun], 'silver'
ARGENTUM.DARE [noun], 'price'
ARHA [postpos.+abl./prev./adv., *arha*], 'forth, away; completely'
ASCIA [noun, **karmal*-?], 'axe'
ASINUS(.ANIMAL) [noun, C., *tarkasna*-], 'donkey; homer'
AUDIRE [v., **tuma(n)ti*-], 'to hear'; PRAE AUDIRE [*paran *tuma(n)ti*-], 'to hear of, about'
AVUS-*ha*- [noun, C., *huha*-], 'grandfather'
AVUS-*hat(i)*- [noun, C., *huhat(i)*-], 'great-grandfather'

BONUS [noun, *wasara*-], 'favour, goodness'
BONUS [adj., *sanawa/i*-], 'good'
BONUS [v., *wasu*-], 'to be good'
BONUS-*ia* [v., *sanawiya*-], 'to be good'
BONUS-*liya*- [v., *waliya*-], 'to exalt'
BONUS-*ma/i*- [adj., *wasama/i*-], 'dear'
BONUS-*saza*- [v., *wasaza*-], 'be dear(?) to'
BONUS(-)*usutara/i*-[v.], 'to benefit(?)'
BOS [noun, C., *wawa/i*-], 'ox'

CAELUM [noun, N., *tipas*-], 'sky, heaven'
CANIS [noun, C., *suwan(i)*-], 'dog'
CAPERE [v., *(la)la*-], 'to take'
CAPERE-*man*- [noun, N.], 'contract, agreement'

CAPUT [noun, C., *harmaha/i-*], 'head'

CAPUT-*ta/i-* [noun, C.], 'man; prince'

CAPUT-*tiya-* [adj.], 'manly; princely'

CASTRUM [noun, N. *harnisa(n)-*], 'fortress'

CENTUM [num.], 'hundred'

CONTRACTUS.DARE [v.], 'to sell'

COR [noun, C., *atri-, atli-, (a)tan(i)-*], 'person, soul'

COR [noun, N., *zart-*], 'heart'

CORNU+CAPUT-*ma/i-* [noun, C., *masanama/i-*], 'one belonging to a god (some kind of priest)'

CRUS [v., *ta-*], 'to stand'; CRUS-*nu(wa)- (tanuwa-)*, 'to make stand, set up'; CRUS + inf. 'to begin to do something'

CRUS [v.], 'to come'; *anta* CRUS, 'to come inside'

CRUS.CRUS [noun, *niyasha-(?)*], 'procession'

CRUS.CRUS [v., *(ni)niya-*], 'to follow'; PRAE-*na* CRUS.CRUS [v.], to pass down'

CRUS+*RA/I* [v., **ar-(?)*], 'to stand; cost'

CULTER [v., *partuni-*], 'to sever(?)'

CUM-*ni/-i* [postpos./prev.], 'together with; against; for'

CURRUS [noun, C., *wara/izana/i-*], 'chariot(ry)'

DARE [v., *piya-*], 'to give'

DELERE-*nu(wa)-* [v.caus.], 'to destroy'; *arha* DELERE [v.], 'to destroy completely; resolve'

DEUS [noun, C., *masana/i-*], 'god'

DEUS.DOMUS(-)*ha(n)ta* [noun, N.], 'temple'

DOMINUS-*na(-i)-ni-* [noun, C.], 'lord'

DOMINUS-*naniy(a)-* [adj.], 'of a lord'

DOMUS [noun, N., *parna-*], 'house'

DOMUS-*ni(-)*DOMINUS-*ni-* [noun], 'house-lord'

DOMUS.SCALA [noun, C., *tawana/i-?*], 'apartment'

DOMUS.SUPER [noun, C., *haristana/i-*], 'upper floors(?)'

EGO [pers.pron., *amu*], 'I'

EUNUCHUS [noun, C., *wasinasa/i-, usinasa/i-*], 'eunuch'

EXERCITUS [noun, N., **kuwalan-*], 'army'

FEMINA [noun, C. **wanat(i)-*], 'woman'

FEMINA-*tiyanta/i-* [adj., **wanatiyant(i)-*], 'female'

FEMINA-*tiyantiya(n)-* [noun, N., **wanatiyantiya-*], 'femininity'

FEMINA.*462* [noun, C., 4-*ta* (*muwita/i-?*)], 'female seed'

FILIA [noun, C., *tuwatar(i)-*], 'daughter'

FINES [noun, C., *irha/i-*], 'border'
FLUMEN [noun, C., **hapa/i-*], 'river'
FLUMEN.DOMINUS-*ia*- [noun], 'river-lord'
FLUMEN.REGIO [noun, C., *hapata/i-*], 'river-land'
FORTIS [adj., *muwatala/i-*], 'mighty, potent'
FRATER-*la*- [noun, C., *atala-*(?)], 'brother'
FRONS [noun, N., *hant-*], 'face'
FRONS-*ti* [postpos., *hanti*], 'in front of, before; against'
FULGUR [noun, N., *pihas-*], 'lightning; victory'
"FUSUS"(-)*sitara/i*- [noun], 'spindle'

GAZELLA [noun, C., *irwa-, sasa-*], 'gazelle'

HEROS [noun, C., **hastala/i-*], 'hero'
HORDEUM [noun, N.], 'barley'

INFANS [noun, C., *nimuwiza-, niwiza-, niza-*], 'son'
INFANS.*NI* [noun, C., *niwarana/i-*], 'son, child'
INFANS.NEPOS [noun, C., *hamsa/i-*], 'grandson'
INFANS.NEPOS [noun, C., *hamsukala-*], 'great-grandson'
INFRA*(-ta)* [prev./postpos., **kata*], 'down, below'
INFRA-*ta-ta* [adv., **katanta*], 'down'
INFRA-*tara/i*- [prev., *anantara/i-*], 'under'
IUDEX [noun, C., *tarwani-*], 'ruler; judge(?)'
IUDEX CAPUT-*ta/i*- [noun, C.], 'prince-ruler(?)'
IUSTITIA [noun, C.? *tarwan(a)-*], 'justice'

LEO(.ANIMAL) [noun, C., **walwa/i-*], 'lion'
LEPUS [noun, C., **tapariya-*], 'authority'
LEPUS [noun, C., **tapariyala-*], 'governor'
LIBARE [noun, N. *sarlata-*], 'libation, offer'
LIBARE [v., *sarl(a)i-, sasarla-*], 'to libate, offer'
LIGNUM [noun, C., *haz(iy)ani-*], 'mayor'
LIGNUM [noun, N., *salha(t)-*], 'succession'
LIGNUM [noun, N., *taru(t)-*], 'wood'
LINGERE [noun, C., *hasa-*(?)], 'luxury'
LINGUA [noun, C., **lalant(i)-*], 'tongue, language'
LIS-*la/i/uhiri*- [noun], 'lawsuit, quarrel, prosecution'
LIS-*saliza-/-lisa*- [v.], 'to litigate'
LITUUS+*na*- [v., **mana-*], 'to see'; *anta* LITUUS+*na*-, 'to behold'; *anan*
 (SUB-*na-na*) LITUUS+*na*-, 'to despise'
LITUUS [v., *tiyari(ya)-*], 'to watch, guard'

LOCUS [noun, N., *pita(nt)*-], 'place; precinct'
LONGUS [adj., *araiy(a)*-], 'long'
LOQUI [v., *tatariya*-], 'to curse'

MAGNUS [adj., *ura/i*-], 'great'
MAGNUS-*ranuwa*- [v., *uranuwa*-], 'make great, promote'
MAGNUS.DOMINA [noun, C., *hasusara*-], 'queen'
MAGNUS.REX [adj.+noun, C., *ura-* **hantawat(i)*-], 'Great King'
MALLEUS [v.], 'to deface'; **arha MALLEUS-*la*-** [v.], 'to destroy'
MALUS [noun, N., *haniyata*-], 'evil'
MALUS(2) [noun, *haniyatastra/i*-], 'evil, badness'
MANUS [noun, C., *istra/i*-], 'hand'
MANUS(-)*latara*- [v.], 'to extend'
ARHA **MANUS(-)*iti*-** [prev.+v.], 'to delete, erase'
MATER [noun, C., **anat(i)*-], 'mother'
MENSA [noun, N., *wasi(ya)*-], 'table'
MILLE [num.], 'thousand'
MONS [noun, C., det.], 'mountain'
MORI [v., *wala-, wara*-], 'to suffer, be ill; *arha* MORI 'to die'

NEG₂ [neg., *na(wa)*], 'not'
NEG₂-*pa* [disj., *napa*], 'or'
NEG₂ **REL-*ha-na*** [neg.+adv., *na kwihan(?)*], 'not at all'
NEG₃ [neg., *nis*], 'not' (prohibitive)
NEG₃-*pa* [disj., *nipa*], 'or'
NEPOS-*ta*- [noun], 'posterity(?)'

OCCIDENS [noun, *ipama*-], 'west'
OMNIS [adj., *tanima/i*-], 'all, every'
ORIENS [noun, *kistama*-], 'east'
OVIS [noun, C., *hawa/i*-], 'sheep'

PANIS [noun, C., *turpa/i*-], 'bread'
PANIS.PITHOS-*ni*- [noun, C.], 'food(?)'
PANIS.PITHOS [noun, N., *azali(ya)*-], 'food, feast'
PES [v., *awi*-], 'to come'; *ARHA* PES, 'to come forth'
PES [noun, C., *pata/i*-], 'foot'
PES₂ [v.], 'to go'; *ARHA* PES₂, 'to go away, die'
PES₂.**PES**₂-*tà*- [v.], 'to go, walk'
PODIUM [noun, *humt(i)*-], 'podium'
PONERE [v., *tuwa*-], 'place, put; establish'
PORTA-*lana*- [noun, N., plural only, **hilana*-(?)], 'gate(s)'

POST-*na/-ni* [prev./postpos.+d./adv., *apan*], 'behind, after; afterwards'
POST+*ra/i*- [adj., **appara/i*-], 'subsequent, younger, inferior'
POST+*ra/i-ta* [adv.], 'hereafter'
POST+*ra/iwa/isati* [adv.], 'afterwards'
PRAE [postpos.+d./prev./adv. *pari*], 'over'
PRAE-*na/-ni* [prev./postpos.+d., *paran*], 'before, in front of'
PRAE-*ti* [postpos.+d., *par(iy)a(n)ti*(?) / *hanti(?)*], 'before'
PUGNUS(-)*la/i/umi*- [v.], 'to strengthen'
PUGNUS(-)*la/i/umitaiy(a)*- [adj.], 'strong'
PUGNUS-*ri*- [v., **ariya-?*], 'to rise, raise; exalt'
PURUS [adj., *kumaiy(a)*-], 'pure, sacred'

REGIO [noun, N., *utni- / det. of GN], 'land, country; people, nation'
REGIO-*ni*(-)DOMINUS [noun, C.], 'Country-Lord'
REL [rel.pron., *kwi*-/ *kwa*-], 'who, which'
REL-*i* [indef.pron., *kwi*], 'kind of'
REL-*i* ... REL [conj.], 'when ... at all(?); whenever(?)'
REL-*iha* [indef.pron., *kwis-ha*], 'someone'
REL-*ita* [adv., *kwita(n)*], 'where'
REL-*ita* REL-*ita* [adv., *kwita(n) kwita(n)*], 'wheresoever'
REL-*pa* [adv., *kwipa*], 'indeed'
REL+*ra/i* [conj., *kwari*], 'as'
REL-*za* [interrogative pron., *kwa(n)za*], 'since; why'
REL-*za* [v., *kwaza*-, log. CAPERE+SCALPRUM], 'to cut'
REX [noun, C., **hantawat(i)*-], 'king'
REX-*tahi(t)*- [noun, N., **hantawatahi(t)*-], 'kingdom, kingship'

SACERDOS [noun, C.], 'priest'
"SCALPRUM" [noun, C., *asu*-], 'stone'
SCALPRUM [noun, C., *kutasara/i*-], 'orthostats'
SCALPRUM [v., *kutasari*-], 'to orthostate (to put up orthostats?)'
SCALPRUM [noun, C., *mana*-], 'mina'
SCALPRUM+*RA/I.LA/I/U* [adj., *warpala/i*-], 'brave'
SCRIBA+*RA/I* [?], '?'
SCRIBA-*la*- [noun, C., **tuppala-?*], 'scribe'
SCRIBA-*laliya*- [noun, N.], 'writing'
SCRIBA-*liya*- [noun], 'writing'
SCUTUM [noun, C., *hara/ila/i*-], 'shield'
SERVUS-*ta₄*- [noun, C.], 'servant'
SOL-*mi(ya)*- [noun, C., *tiwatami(ya)-, tiwarimi(ya)*-], 'offspring of the sun'
SOLIUM(-*MI-*) [v., *asa*-], 'to sit'
SOLIUM-*MI-ia*- [noun, C., **asiya-?*], 'living'

"SOLIUM"(-)*x-ma-ma-* [noun, N.], 'settlements(?)'
SPHINX [noun, C., *awiti-*(?)], 'sphinx'
STATUA [noun, N., *taru(t)-*], 'statue'
STELE [noun, N., *wani(t)-, tanis(a)-*], 'stele'
SUB-*nan* [prev./adv./postpos.+d., *anan*], 'under'
SUPER+*ra/i* [postpos.+d./prev./adv., *sara/i*], 'on, above; up, over';
    SUPER+*ra/i* INFRA-*ta* (*sara/i kata*), 'up (and) down'
SUPER+*ra/i-ta* [postpos.+d., *sara(n)ta*], 'upon'

"TERRA" [noun, C., **taskwira/i-*], 'land, ground, territory'
TERRA+*LA*+*LA* / TERRA+*X* [noun, N., *walilita-, walirita-*], 'field, plain'
THRONUS [noun, N., *istarta-*], 'throne'

"UNUS"-*ta* [num.]. 'at one time(?)'
URBS+*MI-na/i-* [noun, C.], 'city'

VACUUS [adj., *tanata/i-*], 'empty, waste'
VERSUS [postpos.+d., *tawiyan*], 'towards'
VIA [noun, C., *harwa-*], 'road'
VIR [noun, C., **zita/i-*], 'man'
VIR-*tiyant(i)-* [adj., **zitiyant(i)-*], 'male'
VIR-*tiyantiya-* [noun, N., **zitiyantiya-*], 'masculinity'
VITELLUS [noun], 'calf'
VITIS [noun, *tuwarsa-*], 'vineyard'
VITIS [noun, C., *wiyan(a)-*], 'vine'

ARHA **"*69"(-)*iti-*** [v.], 'to delete'
179.SCALPRUM [noun, C.], 'millstone(?)'
190.THRONUS [noun], 'throne'
261.PUGNUS-*ru- [v.], 'to construct(?)'
273 [noun, C., *warpa/i-*], 'courage'
274 [v., *hatal(a)i-*], 'to smite'
336-*nan [postpos.], 'in front of(?)'
348(-)*la/i/utali- [noun, C.], 'ancestors(?)'
455-*liya- [noun, C.], 'assemblage(?)'
462 [noun, C., *muwita-*], 'seed'
464 [adv. / noun, N.pl.?, *hatama-*], 'ruinously / ruins(?)'
ARHA ***501-*ha*** [v.], 'remove from'

Divine names

(DEUS)*atrisuha-*, 'Atrisuhas'

(DEUS)BONUS, 'Grain-God (Kuparmas)'
(DEUS)CERVUS$_{(2)}$, 'Runtiyas; Karhuhas'
 (DEUS)*iya-*, 'Eas'
(DEUS)*karhuha-*, 'Karhuhas'
(DEUS)*ku*+**AVIS**, 'Kubabas'
(DEUS)LUNA+*MI*, 'Moon-God (Armas)'
(DEUS)*pahalati-*, 'Ba'alat'
(DEUS)*sarku-*, 'the Mighty One (Eas)'
(DEUS)SOL, 'Sun-God (Tiwazas)'
(DEUS)TONITRUS, 'Tarhunzas'
(DEUS)VITIS, 'Wine-God (Tipariyas?)'

Personal names

anasi-, 'Anasis'
ashawi-, 'Ashwis'
AVIS-*nu*(-)**466*, 'Arnu-x'
BONUS-*ti-*, 'BONUS-tis'
CERVUS$_2$, 'Runtiyas'
haranawiza-, 'Haranawizas'
huli-, 'Hulis'
kurti-, 'Kurtis'
[I]*la*-**PRAE-VIR**[?]*/la*[?]-, 'Laparizitis(?)'
[I]*larama-*, 'Laramas'
MAGNUS+*ra/i-tami-*, 'Uratamis'
MAGNUS.TONITRUS, 'Ura-Tarhunzas'
muwatali-, 'Muwatalis'
[I]*muwizi-*, 'Muwizis'
parita-, 'Paritas'
pihami-, 'Pihamis'
PRAE-*tà-*, 'Paritas'
ruwa-, 'Ruwas'
suhi-, 'Suhis'
[I]**TONITRUS.***HALPA-pa-***CERVUS**$_2$*-tiya-*, 'Halparuntiyas'
[I]**TONITRUS.***HALPA-paruntiya-*, 'Halparuntiyas'
urahilina-, 'Urahilinas'
uratami-, 'Uratamis'
*x-pa-***VIR-***ti-*, 'X-pa-zitis'

Geographical names

arputa- [det. MONS], 'Mt. Arputa'

CORNU+*RA/I* [det. REGIO, *sura-*], 'Sura'
halpawan(i)-, 'Halabean'
imatu-, 'Hama'
karkamisa- [det. URBS, REGIO], 'Karkamiš'
kurkuma- [det. URBS], 'Gurgum' (Maraş)
laka-, 'Laka'
nikima-, 'Nikima'
sakura- [det. FLUMEN+MINUS], 'Sakura'
TONITRUS.*HALPA-pa*, 'Halab (Aleppo)'

7   Sign List

The following sign list is based on the numbering system of Laroche, 1960b, and follows Marazzi, 1998; In the few instances where *CHLI* uses different values, both are given and the *CHLI* values underlined. While signs which are poorly known and understood are included, drawings of abandoned Laroche numbers have been omitted. Numerals prefixed with an asterisk refer to original Laroche entries, if followed by a bracketed number to a specific variant. Bracketed asterisked numerals refer to abandoned Laroche numbers. A postfixed asterisk indicates a new additional entry, two postfixed asterisks indicate a second new entry. A superscript ^{E} indicates Empire period signs or sign values.

Number	Transliteration	Sign
*1 (*487?)	EGO	
*2	EGO$_2$	
*3	--	, ,
*4	^{E} MONS$_2$, s. *207b	
*5	--	
*6	ADORARE	
*7	EDERE	
*8	BIBERE	

*9 (*444)	AMPLECTI	
*10	CAPUT	
10	CAPUT+SCALPRUM	
*11	--	
*12	STATUA	
*13	^E, s. *14	
*14 (*13)	PRAE; *pari*	
*15	DOMINA	
*16	MAGNUS.DOMINA	
*17	REX	
*18	MAGNUS.REX	
*19	*á*	
*20	(LITUUS)*á* / LITUUS+*Á*, LITUUS+*á*	

*21	HEROS	
*22	LOQUI	
*23	LIS(?)	
*24	LIS	
*25	OCULUS	
*26 (*113)	FRONS	
*27	LIBARE	
*28	FORTIS	
*29	^E*TÁ, tá*	
*30	--	
*31	LIGARE (PUGNUS+PUGNUS)	
*32	BRACCHIUM	
*33	--	
*34	POST	

*35	*na*	
*36	LITUUS+*na*	
*37	--	
*38	--	
*39 (*40, *44?)	PUGNUS	
39	PUGNUS+X	
*40	s. *39	
*41	CAPERE; *tà*	
*42	CAPERE$_2$.CAPERE$_2$, *ta*$_x$	
*43 (*136)	CAPERE$_2$	
*44	s. *39 / *59?	
*45	INFANS, FILIUS, FRATER	
45	FILIA	
*46	REX.INFANS, REX.FILIUS	

46	^EREX.FILIA	
*46**	^EMAGNUS.FILIA	
*47	--	
*48	--	
*49	*a-tá* / *a+tá*	
*50	--	
*51	PUGNUS.URBS	
*52	MANUS.CULTER	
*53	^EENSIS, ^EMANUS+CULTER	
*54	--	
*55	^E*nì*	
*56	^EINFRA, ^ESUB, ^E*ká*	
*57 (*56)	INFRA, SUB	
*58	CUM	

*59 (*44?, *60)	MANUS	
*60	s. *59	
*61	MANUS+*218	
*62 (*68)	LONGUS (MANUS+MINUS)	
*63	s. *69	
*64	s. *69	
*65	PONERE	
*66	DARE; *pi*	
66	^EMANDARE (DARE.DARE)	
*66**	^EMANDARE₂	
*67	--	
*68	s. *62	
*69 (*63, *64)	s. *59 (*60)	
*70	SUPER	
*71	--	

*72	--
*73 (*170)	AUDIRE (AURIS+*TU*+*MI*)
*74	--
*75	--
*76	s. *221
*77	--
*78	ALA
*79 (*408)	FEMINA, MATER
*80 (*81)	*SARMA, SARMA₂*
*81	s. *80
*82	CRUS; *ta*₆
*83	CRUS+FLUMEN
*84	CRUS₂; *nà*
*85	GENUFLECTERE; in TONITRUS.*85(-*pa*) = *HALPA*
*86 (*87)	CRUS.CRUS

*87	s. *86	
*88	^E*tu*	
*89	*tu*	
*90	PES; *ti*	
*91 (*92, *94)	PES.SCALA.ROTAE	
*92	s. *91	
*93	PES₂	
*94	s. *91	
*95	PES₂.PES₂	
*96	PES₂.PES	
*97	a) LEO, BESTIA, b) LEO₂	
*98	a) CANIS, b) CANIS₂	
*99	EQUUS	
*100 (*116)	ASINUS; *ta*	
*101	ASINUS₂	

*102	<u>CERVUS</u> / a) CERVUS, b) CERVUS₂; *rú*	a) b)
*103	<u>CERVUS₂</u> / CERVUS₃; *rú*	
*104	<u>GAZELLA</u> / a) CAPRA, b) CAPRA₂, c) CAPRA_{2A}; *sà*	a) , b) c)
*105	<u>BOS</u> / a) BOS b) BOS₂; *u*	a) , b)
*106	--	
*107 (*167)	a) BOS+*MI*, b) BOS.*MI*, c) BOS₂.*MI*; *mu*	a) , b) c)
*108	CORNU; *sú*	
*109	VITELLUS (<u>MA_x</u> in MA_x-LI_x-zi, 'Malatya')	
*110	*ma*	,
*111 (*518?)	a) OVIS, b) OVIS₂ (=*518?)	a) b)

*112   LINGERE; za_4

*113   s. *26

*114   = LITUUS+u

*115 (*124)   <u>LEPUS</u>; *tapa* / a) LEPUS,
b) LEPUS$_2$

a)   b)

*116 ^{E}s. *100

*117   --

*118   --

*119   s. *246

*120   GRYLLUS

*121   SPHINX

*122   --

*123   --

*124   s. *115b

*125 (*126, *457(1))   *li*

125   UNGULA; *(<u>LI</u>$_x$* in *MA$_x$-
LI$_x$-zi*, 'Malatya')

*126 (*457(1))	s. *125	
*127	[decoration only]	
*128	AVIS; zi_4	
*129	--	
*130	$AVIS_3$	
*131	$^{E}AVIS_5$	
*132	$AVIS_2$	
*133 (*134)	AQUILA ($AVIS_4$); ara/i	
*134	ara/i, s. *133	
*135	$^{E}AVIS_x$	
*136	s. *43	
*137	$^{E}LIBATIO$	
*138	PISCIS	
*139	--	
*140	--	

*141	--	
*142	--	
*143	s. *214	
*144	--	
*145	--	
*146	--	
*147	--	
*148	ᴱIANUS	
*149	--	
*150	--	
*151	ᴱ*TELIPINU*	
*152	--	
*153	*nu*	
*154	--	
*155	--	
*156	--	

*157	--	
*158	--	
*159	--	
*160	VITIS; $^E wi$	
*161	--	
*162	--	
*163	--	
*164	--	
*165 (*320)	BONUS; *wà/ì*	
*166	*wá/ì*	
*167	s. *107	
*168	s. *329	
*169	s. *382	
*170	s. *73	
*171	--	
*172	*ta₅/i₅* or *lá/i*	

*173	^EHASTARIUS	
*174	*si*	
*175	LINGUA; *la*	
*176	*LA+LA*	
*177	^ELINGUA+CLAVUS	
*178	*la+ra+a*	
*179 (*453, *454)	HORDEUM; *hwi_x*	
*180	--	
*181	PANIS; *HALA*; *pa_x*	
*182	CAELUM	
*183	s. *423	
*184	--	
*185	--	
*186	^E, s. *445	
*187	--	
*188	--	
*189	--	
*190	SOL₂	

*191 (*465, *467)	SOL	
*192	ORIENS	
*193	LUNA	
*194	--	
*195	--	
*196	^{E}*HATTI*; *há*	
*197	^{E}*HATTI*+*li*; <u>*HÁ*+*LI*</u>	
*198	--	
*199	TONITRUS	
*200	FULGUR	
*201	TERRA, LOCUS, *wa*/*i*$_6$	
*202	a) VIA+TERRA. SCALPRUM, b) VIA+TERRA+ SCALPRUM, c) ^{E}(DEUS)VIA+TERRA	a) b) c)
*203	--	
*204	*wa*/*i*$_5$	
*205	--	
*206	--	

*207 (*4)   <u>MONS</u> / a) MONS, b)
                             MONS₂;
                             wa/i₄

a)   b)

207   ᴱLEO+MONS.*TU*+LEO

*208   --

*209   i (ᴱi(a))

*210   ia

*211   --

*212 (*213)   FLUMEN

*213   s. *212

*214 (*143)   ní

*215   a) FONS; b) ha

a)   b)

*216   a) FINES, *ARHA*
                             b) (FINES+ha =) *ARHA*
                             c) ᴱ*216

a)   b)

c)

*217   --

*218   --

*219   --

*220	--	
*221 (*76, *222)	VIA	
*222	s. *221	
*223	sa_6	
*224	ha?/ pa?	
*225	URBS	
*226	^E*IŠUWA*(URBS)	
*227	a) URBS+*RA/I-li* b) URBS+*li;* URBS-*li*	
*228 (*230)	REGIO; tu_4	
*229	*MÍ*.REGIO	
*230	REGIO; tu_4	
*231 (*232, *233)	CASTRUM	
*232	s. *231	
*233	s. *231	
*234	--	

*235	TURRIS?	
*236	MURUS?	
*237 (*238)	PORTA	
*238	s. *237	
*239	PORTA₂	
*240	--	
*241	_ki₄_ / _kiₓ_	
*242	s. *432	
*243	CUBITUM	
*244	AEDIFICIUM	
*245 (*359(2))	VACUUS (AEDIFICIUM+MINUS)	
*246 (*119)	AEDIFICARE (AEDIFICIUM.PONERE)	
*247	DOMUS	
*248	DELERE (DOMUS+MINUS)	
*249	DEUS.DOMUS	
*250	ᴱMAGNUS.DOMUS	

*251	DOMUS+X	
*252 (*253)	DOMUS+SCALA	
*253	s. *252	
*254	^{E}EUNUCHUS$_2$	
*255 (*256)	HORREUM?	
*256	s. *255	
*257 (*258, *260)	ARGENTUM	
*258	s. *257	
*259	--	
*260	s. *257	
*261	--	
*262	--	
*263	--	
*264	PODIUM	
*265	--	
*266	= PES.REGIO	
*267	STELE (LAPIS+SCALPRUM)	
267	LAPIS	

*268	SCALPRUM	
*269	EXERCITUS	
*270	^E, s. *70	
*271	*TAWANANNA*	
*272	SCUTUM	
*273	--	
*274	--	
*275	--	
*276	^EFRATER₂	
*277	IUSTITIA.*LA*, IUDEX.*LA*, *371.*LA* / <u>IUDEX+*la*</u>	
*278	*li*	
*279	--	
*280	MALLEUS; *wa/i₉*	
*281	ASCIA	
*282	*HAH(A)(?)*	

*283	*TUZZI*(?)	
*284	*TUZZI*(?)	
*285	^E*zu(wa)*?	
*286	*wa/i₇*	
*287	s. *399	
*288	CURRUS	
*289	^EAURIGA	
*290	*hara/i*	
*291	*lì*	
*292	ROTA, ^E*HALA/I*	
*293	--	
*294	THRONUS/MENSA	
294	THRONUS/MENSA₂ (= *SARPA*)	
*295	SOL₂.THRONUS/MENSA (*190.THRONUS)	
*296 (*297?)	^EMONS.MENSA / MONS.*SARPA*	

*283   *TUZZI*(?)

*284   *TUZZI*(?)

*285 $^{E}zu(wa)$?

*286 wa/i_7

*287   s. *399

*288   CURRUS

*289 ^{E}AURIGA

*290   *hara/i*

*291   *lì*

*292   ROTA, ^{E}*HALA/I*

*293   --

*294   THRONUS/MENSA

294   THRONUS/MENSA$_2$ (= *SARPA*)

*295   SOL$_2$.THRONUS/MENSA (*190.THRONUS)

*296 (*297?) ^{E}MONS.MENSA / MONS.*SARPA*

*297	s. *296?	
*298	THRONUS₂	
*299	SOLIUM; *i* (+ *450 = *iá*)	
*300		
(*45+)*300+*488	NEPOS (= ᴱ*59+*300)	
*301	LECTUS	
*302	s. *399	
*303	*SARA/I; sara/i*	
*304	*mà*	
*305	FUSUS	
*306	ᴱ*hí*	
*307 (*342)	*hu*	
*308	--	
*309	CRUX	
*310	= *201?	
*311	--	

*312	^E, s. *313	
*313 (*312)	VIR; *zí*	
*314	log.; *ha*$_x$	
*315	*kar*	
*316	*sa*$_7$	
*317	--	
*318	^E*TEŠUB*; *TASU*(?)	
*319 (*339, *416)	*ta*$_4$/*i*$_4$ or *la*/*i*	
*320	^E, s. *165	
*321	--	
*322 (*323)	PURUS	
*323	s. *322	
*324	--	
*325	*tú*	
*326	SCRIBA; *tù*	
*327	SIGILLUM; *sa*$_5$	

*328	*pu*	
*329	REL; *kwi/a*	
329	s. *508	
*330	CAPERE+SCALPRUM	
*331	AVUS	
*332a	NEG	
*332b	NEG₂; *ná*	
*332c	NEG₃	
*333	--	
*334	*pa*	
*335	*zá*	
*336	ANNUS (PITHOS. SCUTELLA / PITHOS); *zì*; *336+*450 = *za*ₓ,	
336	*378+*336 = *zà*	
*337	PITHOS	
*338	CULTER	
*339	s. *319	

*340	ANNUS+ANNUS	
*341	COR	
*342	s. *307	
*343	s. *337	
*344	CONTRACTUS	
*345 (*352, *353, *354, *519?)	URCEUS	
*346	POCULUM	
*347	*hú*	
*348	s. *349	
*349 (*348)	--	
*350	--	
*351	--	
*352	[E], s. *345	
*353	[E], s. *345	
*354	[E], s. . *345	
*355	SACERDOS	

*356	--	
*357	--	
*358 (*359(1))	DIES	
*359(1)	s. *358	
*359(2)	s. *245	
*360	DEUS	
*361	--	
*362	*má*	
*363	MAGNUS, ^EUR / ^E<u>ur</u>	
*364	a) *u*, b) *mu*	a) ... b) ...
*365	--	
*366	OMNIS	
*367	^E<u>TALA</u>, TAL	
*368	MALUS	
368	MALUS₂	
*369	^EVITA	
*370	^EBONUS₂; *su*	
*371	IUDEX, IUSTITIA; (*371+*383 = IUDEX+*RA/I*; *tara/i*_x)	

*372	^{E}SACERDOS$_2$	
*373	--	
*374	= *216?	
*375	--	
*376	zi ($^E zi/a$)	
*377	za	
*378	LITUUS	
*379	OCCIDENS; $ià$	
*380	UNUS; sa_8; ^{I} [determinative of personal names]	
*381	MINUS	
381	MORI (VIR$_2$.MINUS)	
*382 (*169)	LIGNUM	
*383	$+ra/i$	
*384	"2"	
*385	"2"(?)	
*386	^{E}VIR$_2$; | [word divider]	
*387	SERVUS; $mì$	

*388	"3"	
*389	*tara/i*	
*390	DOMINUS	
*391	"4"; *mi*	
*392	"5"	
*393 (*394?)	"8"	
*394	= *393?	
*395	"9"; *nú*	
*396	--	
*397	DECEM	
*398	--	
*399 (*287, *302)	CENTUM	
*400	MILLE	
*401	s. *477	
*402	SCUTELLA; *sa₄*	
*403	--	
*404	ANIMAL	
*405	--	
*406	--	
*407	--	
*408	[E], s. *79	

*409	--	
*410	" " [logogram markers]	
*411	*ni*	
*412	*ru*	
*413	*hi*	
*414	^E*hi*	
*415	*sa*	
*416	^E, s. *319	
*417	*sa*_x	
*418	*318+*MI*	
*419 (*420)	^E*URHI*; RHOMBUS; *mí*	
*420	s. *419	
*421	^E*US*	
*422	PANIS.SCUTELLA	
*423 (*183)	*ku*	
*424	--	
*425	--	
*426	--	
*427	--	

*428	--	
*429	*TANA*	
*430	OMNIS$_2$; *pú*	
*431	--	
*432 (*242)	*za$_5$*	
*433	*sá*	
*434	*ka*	
*435	*a$_x$*?	
*436	--	
*437	--	
*438	^{E}PASTOR	
*439	*wa/i*	
*440	--	
*441	--	
*442	--	
*443	--	
*444	s. *9	
*445	*la/i/u*; ^{E}*lu*	
*446	*ki*	

*447

      *447.*26   VERSUS; ni_x

*448   *zú*

*449   --

*450   *a, ' *[space filler(?)]

*451   [E]*hur*, HUR

*452   --

*453   s. *179
*454   s. *179
*455 la_x

*456   *sí*?

*457(1)   s. *125
*457(2)   --

*458   --

*459   --

*460   --

*461	--	
*462	ma_x	
*463	--	
*464	--	
*465	s. *191	
*466	--	
*467	s. *191	
*468	s. *469	
*469 (*468)	--	
*470	"12" (10+2)	
*471	--	
*472	--	
*473	s. *474	
*474 (*473)	EUNUCHUS	
*475	--	

*476	--	
*477 (*401, *479)	FLAMMAE(?)	
*478	--	
*479	s. *477	
*480	--	
*481	--	
*482	--	
*483	--	
*484	--	
*485	--	
*486	FALX(?)	
*487	s. *1?	
*488	*tí*	
*300 + *488	NEPOS, s.*300	
*489	--	
*490	--	
*491	--	
*492	--	

*493   --

*494   --

*495   --

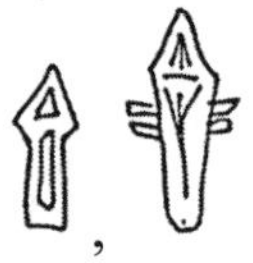

*496   --

*497   --

*501   --

*502   --

*503   --

*504   --

*505   --

*506   *HANA*

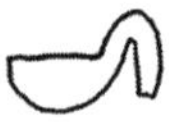

*507   --

*508 (*329*)   CURRERE; *HWI;hwi/a*

*509   --

*510   --

*511	--	
*512	--	
*513	--	
*514	--	
*515	--	
*516	--	
*517	--	
*518	s. *111?	
*519	s. *345?	
*520	--	
*521	--	
*522	--	
*523	--	
*524	PROPHETA? (CORNU+CAPUT)	
*525	PRINCEPS	

*526   ^E*ti*

9 Bibliography

d'Alfonso, L.
- 2012a. Notes on Anatolian Hieroglyphic Palaeography: An Investigation of the Sign *439, *wa/wi*, in: P. Coticelli Kurras et al. (eds.), *Interferenze linguistiche e contatti culturali in Anatolia tra II e I millennio a.C., Studi in onore di Onofrio Carruba in occasione del suo 80° compleanno*, Pavia, 81–100.
- 2012b, Tabal, an 'Out-Group Definition' in the 1st Millennium BC, in: G.B. Lanfranchi et al. (eds.), *Leggo! Festschrift F.M. Fales*, Wiesbaden, 173–194.

Arbeitman, Y.,
- 1977. Cuneiform and Hieroglyphic Luwian *–za*, *KZ* 90, 145–148.

Bossert, H. Th.,
- 1932. Šantaš und Kubaba, *MAOG* 6/3, Leipzig.
- 1960. Ist die B-L Schrift im wesentlichen entziffert?, *Or* 29, 423–432
- 1961a. Die Entzifferung der B-L Schrift wird fortgesetzt, *Or* 30, 110–118.
- 1961b. Zur Vokalisation des Luwischen, *Or* 30, 314–322.

Bryce, T.,
- 1998. *The Kingdom of the Hittites*, Oxford.
- 2003. History, in: Melchert, 2003, 27–127.
- 2012. The World of the Neo-Hittite Kingdoms. A Political and Military History, Oxford.

Çambel, H.,
- 1999. Corpus of Hieroglyphic Luwian Inscriptions, Volume II. *Karatepe-Aslantaş. The Inscriptions: Facsimile Edition*, Berlin/New York.

Carruba, O.,
- 1979. Sui numerali da "1" a "5" in anatolico e indoeuropeo, *Fs Szemerényi*, 191–205.
- 1982. Der Kasus auf *-sa* des Luwischen, *Gs Kronasser*, Wiesbaden, 1–15.
- 1984. Nasalisation im Anatolischen, *SMEA* 24, 57–69.
- 1985. Die anatolischen Partikeln der Satzeinleitung, in: Schlerath, B. (ed.), Grammatische Kategorien, *Akten der VII. Fachtagung der Indogermanischen Gesellschaft*, Berlin 20.-25. Februar 1983, Wiesbaden, 79–98.
- 1986. Die 3. Pers. Sing. des Possessivpronomens im Luwischen, *Fs Güterbock*, 49–52.

- 1998. Geroglifico anatolico 1995: note conclusive alla giornata di studio, in: Marazzi, 1998, 267–283.

Charles, B.B.,
- 1911. *Hittite Inscriptions*, Ithaca/New York.

Collon, D. and George, A.,
- 2010. (ed.) Iraq 72. In honour of the seventieth birthday of Professor David Hawkins.

Coticelli Kurras, P.
- 2000. Zum hethitischen Komparativ, in: Ofitsch, M. and Zinko, Chr. (ed.), *125 Jahre Indogermanistik in Graz*, Graz , 33–45.

Crossland, R.A. and Birchall, A.,
- 1973 (ed.). Bronze Age Migrations in the Aegean, London.

Dinçol, A. and Dinçol, B.,
- 2008. *Die Prinzen- und Beamtensiegel aus der Oberstadt von Boğazköy -Hattusa vom 16. Jahrhundert bis zum Ende der Großreichszeit*, Boğazköy-Hattusa 22, Mainz.

Eichner, H.,
- 1985. *Malwa*, eine hieroglyphenluvisch-sidetische Wortgleichung, *MSS* 45, 5–21.

Forrer, E.,
- 1932. *Die hethitische Bilderschrift*, SAOC 3, Chicago.

Friedrich, J.,
- 1939. *Entzifferungsgeschichte der hethitischen Hieroglyphenschrift*, Stuttgart.
- 1954. *Entzifferung verschollener Schriften*, Berlin-Göttingen-Heidelberg.
- 1958. Hochsprache und Umgangssprache im Bildhethitischen?, in: *Fs Krahe*, 45–48.

Gelb, I.J.,
- 1931, 1935, 1942. *Hittite Hieroglyphs I, II, III*, SAOC 2, 14, 21, Chicago.

Giusfredi, F.
- 2009. The Problem of the Luwian Title *tarwanis*. AoF 36, 140–145.
- 2010. *Sources for a Socio-Economic History of the Neo-Hittite States*. Texte der Hethiter 28. Heidelberg.

Goedegebuure, P.,
- 2007. The Hieroglyphic Luwian demonstrative ablative-instrumentals *zin* and *apin*, in: Archi, A. and Francia, R. (eds.), Atti del 6o Congresso di Ittitologia, SMEA 49/1, 319–334.

Güterbock, H.G.,
- 1940. *Siegel aus Boğazköy, 1. Teil*, AfO Bh. 5, Berlin.
- 1942. *Siegel aus Boğazköy, 2. Teil*, AfO Bh. 7, Berlin.

Hajnal, I.

- 2000. Der adjektivische Genitivausdruck der luwischen Sprachen (im Lichte neuerer Erkenntnis), in: Ofitsch, M. and Zinko, Chr. (ed.), *125 Jahre Indogermanistik in Graz*, Graz, 159-184.

Hawkins, J. D.,

- 1975. The Negatives in Hieroglyphic Luwian, *AnSt* 25, 119–156.
- 1982. The neo-Hittite States in Syria and Anatolia, in: Boardman, J. (ed.), *CAH*, Vol. III, part I, 372–441.
- 1986. Writing in Anatolia. Imported and Indigenous Systems, *World Archaeology* 17, 363–376.
- 2000. Corpus of Hieroglyphic Luwian Inscriptions, Volume I, *Inscriptions of the Iron Age*, Berlin/New York.
- 2002. Anatolia: The End of the Hittite Empire and after, in: Braun-Holzinger, E.A. and Matthäus, H. (ed.), *Die nahöstlichen Kulturen und Griechenland an der Wende vom 2. zum 1. Jahrtausend v. Chr.*, Möhnesee-Wamel.
- 2003. Scripts and Texts, in Melchert (ed.) 2003, 128–169.
- 2004. "The Stag-God of the Countryside and Related Problems". In: Penney, J.H.W. (ed.), *Indo-European Perspectives, Studies in Honour of Anna Morpurgo Davies*, Oxford: 355-369.
- 2006. The Inscription, in: Bunnens, G. , Hawkins, J. D. and Leirens, I., *Tell Ahmar: New Luwian Stele and the Cult of the Storm-God at Til Barsib-Masuwari Pt. 2*, Publications De La Mission Archeologique De L'Universite De Liege En Syrie, Louvain, 11–32.
- 2011. The Inscriptions of the Aleppo Temple, *AnSt* 61: 35-54.

Hawkins, J.D. and Morpurgo Davies, A.,

- 1975. Hieroglyphic Hittite: Some New Readings and their Consequences, *JRAS* 76, 121–133.
- 1993. Running and Relatives in Luwian, *Kadmos* 32, 50–60.
- 2010. More Negatives and Disjunctives in Hieroglyphic Luwian, in: Kim et al. 2010, 98–128.

Hawkins, J.D., Morpurgo Davies, A. and Neumann, G.,

- 1974. *Hittite Hieroglyphs and Luwian: New Evidence for the Connection*, Nachrichten der Akademie der Wissenschaften in Göttingen, I. Philologisch-historische Klasse, Göttingen.

Heinhold-Krahmer, S.,

- 1977. *Arzawa – Untersuchungen zu seiner Geschichte nach den hethitischen Quellen*, Heidelberg

Herbordt, S.,

- 2005. *Die Prinzen- und Beamtensiegel der hethitischen Gro"reichszeit auf Tonbullen aus dem Nisantepe-Archiv in Hattusa*, Boğazköy-Hattusa 19, Mainz.

Herbordt, S., Bawanypeck, D., and Hawkins, J.D.,
- 2011. *Die Siegel der Grosskönige und Grossköniginnen auf Tonbullen aus dem Nişantepe-Archiv in Hattusa*, Boğazköy-Hattuša 23, Mainz.

Hoffner, H.A. and Melchert, H.C.,
- 2007. *A Grammar of the Hittite Language*, Winona Lake.

van den Hout, Th.,
- 1984. Einige luwische Neutra auf *-sa/-za* in überwiegend junghethitischen Texten, *KZ* 97, 60–80.
- 2002. Self, Soul and Portrait in Hieroglyphic Luwian, in Taracha, P. (ed.), *Silva Anatolica. Anatolian Studies Presented to Maciej Popko on the Occasion of His 65th Birthday*, Warsaw 2002, 171–186.
- 2006. Institutions, Vernaculars, Publics: the Case of Second-Millennium Anatolia, in Sanders, S. (ed.), Margins of Writing, Origins of Cultures, Chicago, 217–56.
- 2010. The Hieroglyphic Signs L. 255/256 and KARATEPE XI. In: Singer, I. (ed*.) ipamati kistamati pari tumatimis, Luwian and Hittite Studies presented to J. David Hawkins on the occasion of his 70th birthday*, Emery and Claire Yass Publications in Archaeology, Institute of Archaeology, Tel Aviv University, Tel Aviv, 234–243.

Houwink ten Cate, Ph.H.J.
- 1966. The Ending *-d* of the Hittite Possessive Pronoun, *RHA* 24, Fasc. 79, 123–132.

Hrozny, B.,
- 1933, 1934, 1937. *Les inscriptions hittites hiéroglyphiques, I, II, III,* Prague.

Jasink, A. M.,
- 1995. *Gli stati neo-hittiti. Analisi delle fonti scritte e sintesi storica*, SMEA 10, Pavia.

Kim, R., Oettinger, N., Rieken, E. and Weiss, M.,
- 2010. Ex Anatolia Lux. Anatolian and Indo-European studies in honor of H. Craig Melchert on the occasion of his sixty-fifth birthday. Ann Arbor–New York.

Kloekhorst, A.,
- 2004. The Preservation of *h1 in Hieroglyphic Luwian. Two Separate *a*-Signs, HS 117, 26–49.
- 2006. Initial Laryngeals in Anatolian, HS 119, 77–108.

Laroche, E.,
- 1957/58, 1960a, 1967. Comparaison du louvite et du lycien, *BSL* 53, 159-197; 55, 155-185; 62, 46-66.
- 1960b. *Les hiéroglyphes hittites, Première partie, L'écriture*, Paris.
- 1966. *Les Noms des Hittites*, Paris.

Makkay, J.,
- 1993. *Pottery Links between Late Neolithic Cultures of the NW Pontic and Anatolia, and the Origins of the Hittites*, Anatolica 19.

Marazzi, M.,
- 1990. *Il Geroglifico Anatolico, Problemi di Analisi e Prospettive di Ricerca*, Rome.
- 1994. Ma gli Hittiti scriveveano veramente su 'legno'? in Cipriano, P., Di Giovine, P., Mancini, M. (eds.) *Miscellanea di studi linguistici in onore di Walter Belardi*, Rome: 131–160.
- 1998 [2000]. *Il Geroglifico Anatolico, Sviluppi della ricerca a venti anni dalla sua "ridecifrazione"*, Naples.
- 2007. Sigilli, sigillature e tavolette di legno: alcune considerazioni alla luce di nuovi dati. In: Alparslan, M., Doğan-Alparslan, M. and Peker, H. (eds.), *Belkıs Dinçol ve Ali Dinçol'a Armağan. VITA. Festschrift in Honor of Belkıs Dinçol and Ali Dinçol*. İstanbul: 465–474.

Mazzoni, S.,
- 1981. Gli stati siro-ittiti e l'"età oscura": fatti geo-economici di uno sviluppo culturale, *Egitto e Vicino Oriente* IV, 311–341
- 1982. Gli stati siro-ittiti e l'"età oscura", II. sviluppi iconografici e propaganda politica, *Egitto e Vicino Oriente* V, 197–216.
- 1994 (ed.). *Nuove Fondazioni nel Vicino Oriente Antico: realtità e ideologica*, Pisa.

Melchert, C.,
- 1987. Proto-Indo-European Velars in Luvian, *Studies Cowgill*, 182–204.
- 1988a. Luvian Lexical notes, *HS* 101, 211–243.
- 1988b. "Thorn" and "Minus" in Hieroglyphic Luvian Orthography, *AnSt* 38, 29-42.
- 1990. Adjective Stems in *-iyo-* in Anatolian, *HS* 103, 198–207.
- 1993. *Cuneiform Luvian Lexicon*, Lexica Anatolica 2, Chapel Hill.
- 1994. *Anatolian Historical Phonology*, Amsterdam/Atlanta.
- 1996. Anatolian Hieroglyphs, in: Daniels, P.T. and Bright, W. (ed.), *The World's Writing Systems*, New York/Oxford, 120–124.
- 2002. Covert Possessive Compounds in Hittite and Luvian, in: F. Cavoto (ed.), The Linguist's Linguist: A Collection of Papers in Honour of Alexis Manaster Ramer, München 2002, 297–302.
- 2003 (ed.). *The Luwians*, HdO 68, Leiden/Boston.
- 2004a. Hieroglyphic Luvian Verbs in *-min(a)*, in A. Hyllested (et al. ed.) *Per Aspera ad Asteriskos. Studia Indogermanica in honorem Jens Elmegård Rasmussen sexagenarii Idibus Martiis anno MMIV*, 355–362.

- 2004b. The Inflections of Some Irregular Luvian Neuter Nouns, in: Groddek, D. and Rößle, S. (eds.), *Šarnikzel. Hethitologische Studien zum Gedenken an Emil Orgetorix Forrer*, Dresden, 471–475.
- 2011. Enclitic Subject Pronouns in Hieroglyphic Luvian, in: *Aramazd. Armenian Journal of Near Eastern Studies* 6.2, 73–86.

Mellaart, J.,
- 1966. *The Chalcolithic and Early Bronze Age in the Near East and Anatolia*, Beirut.

Meriggi, P.,
- 1933. Die "hethitischen" Hieroglypheninschriften. I. Die kürzeren Votiv und Bauinschriften, *WZKM* 40, 233–280.
- 1934a. II. Die längeren Votiv und Bauinschriften, *WZKM* 41, 1–42.
- 1934b. Die längsten Bauinschriften in hethitischen Hieroglyphen nebst Glossar zu sämtlichen Texten, *MVAeG* 39/1, 1–77.
- 1962. *Hieroglyphisch-Hethitisches Glossar*, Wiesbaden.
- 1966. *Manuale di Eteo Geroglifico, Parte I - Grammatica*, Rome.
- 1967. *Manuale di Eteo Geroglifico, Parte II - Testi - 1a Serie*, Rome.
- 1975a. *Manuale di Eteo Geroglifico, Parte II - Testi - 2a E 3a Serie*, Rome.
- 1975b. *Manuale di Eteo Geroglifico, Parte II - Tavole - 2a E 3a Serie*, Rome.
- 1980. *Schizzo grammaticale dell'Anatolico*, AANL, Serie 8, Vol. 24/3, 243–409.

Messerschmidt, L.,
- 1900, 1902, 1906. *Corpus Inscriptionum Hettiticarum, Erster Nachtrag, Zweiter Nachtrag*, MVAG 5/4-5, 7/3, 11/5, Berlin.

Mittelberger, H.,
- 1962. Review of Laroche 1960b, *Sprache* 8, 276–286.
- 1963. Bemerkungen zu Meriggis hieroglyphisch-hethitischem Glossar, *Sprache* 9, 69–107.
- 1964. Zur Schreibung und Lautung des Hieroglyphen-luwischen, *Sprache* 10, 50–98.
- 1966. Genitiv und Adjektiv in den altanatolischen Sprachen, *Kratylos* 11, 99–106.

Mora, C.,
- 1991. Sull'origine della scrittura geroglifica anatolica, *Kadmos* 30, 1–28.
- 1994. L'étude de la glyptique anatolienne. Bilan et nouvelles orientations de la recherche, *Syria* 71, 205–215.
- 1995. I Luvi e la scrittura geroglifica anatolica, in: Carruba, O., Giorgieri, M., Mora, C. (ed.), *Atti del II Congresso Internazionale di Hittitologia*, Pavia, 28 giugno - 2 lulio 1993, Pavia.

Mora, C., and d'Alfonso, L.,
-   2012. Anatolia After the End of the Hittite Empire. New Evidence from Southern Cappadocia. Origini 34: 385–398.
Morpurgo Davies, A.,
-   1975. Negation and Disjunction in Anatolian and elsewhere, *AnSt* 25, 157–168.
-   1979. The Luwian Languages and the Hittite -*fi* Conjugation, *Fs Szemerényi*, 577–610.
-   1980a. Analogy and the -*an* Datives of the Hieroglyphic Luwian, *AnSt* 30, 123–137.
-   1980b. The Personal Endings of the Hieroglyphic Luwian Verb, *KZ* 94, 86–108.
-   1982/83. Dentals, Rhotacism and Verbal Endings in the Luwian Languages, *KZ* 96, 245–270.
Mouton, A., Rutherford, I., and Yakubovich, I., (eds.),
-   2013. Luwian Identities. Culture, Language and Religion Between Anatolia and the Aegean. Brill.
Neumann, G.,
-   1965. Das hieroglyphen-luwische Nominalsuffix -*str*-, *Sprache* 11, 82–88.
-   1973. Der Silbenwert "*ya*" in den hethitischen Hieroglyphen, *Fs Otten*, 243–251.
-   1982. Die Konstruktion mit Adjectiva genetivalia in den luwischen Sprachen, *GS Kronasser*, 149–161.
-   1985. Hethitisch-luwische Wortstudien und Etymologien IV, *KZ* 98, 20–25.
-   1992. System und Ausbau der hethitischen Hieroglyphenschrift, Nachrichten der Akademie der Wissenschaften in Göttingen, I. Philologisch-historische Klasse, Göttingen.
-   1996. Hethitisch-luwische Verwandtschaftswörter, *Sprache* 38/1, 1–13.
-   2004. Hieroglyphen-luwisch "reiten", *HS* 117, 22–25.
Nowicki, H.,
-   2000. Zum Einleitungsparagraphen des Anitta-Textes (CTH 1, 1-4), in: Ofitsch, M. and Zinko, Chr. (ed.), *125 Jahre Indogermanistik in Graz*, Graz, 347–356.
Oettinger, N.,
-   1976. Zum Wort- und Bilderschatz der luwischen Sprachen, *MSS* 34, 101–107.
-   1976/77. Nochmals zum lykischen Plural, *IncLing* 3/2, 131–135.
-   1978. Die Gliederung des anatolischen Sprachgebiets, *KZ* 92, 74–92.
-   1987. Bemerkungen zur anatolischen i-Motion und Genusfrage, *KZ* 100, 35–43

- 2002a. *Die Stammbildung des hethitischen Verbums²*, DBH 7, Dresden.
- 2002b. Indogermanische Sprachträger lebten schon im 3. Jahrtausend v. Chr. in Kleinasien, in: *Die Hethiter und ihr Reich – Das Volk der 1000 Götter*, Bonn, 50–55.

Oshiro, T.,
- 1983. The relatives in Hieroglyphic Luwian, *Orient* XIX, 51–61.
- 2000. Hieroglyphic Luwian *tuwati* and *u(n)zati*, GS Carter, 189–193.

Payne, A.
- 2003. Das Schrifttum der Hethiter, in: Seipel, W. (ed.), *Der Turmbau zu Babel*, Band IIIA: Schrift, 111–117.
- 2007. 'Multilingual Inscriptions - Signs of Power or Weakness?' in: Seth L. Sanders (Hg.), Margins of Writing, Origins of Cultures, Oriental Institute Seminars (OIS), 2. edition, 125–140.
- 2008. 'Writing Systems and Identity', in Collins, B.J., Bachvarova, M.R. and Rutherford, I.C. (ed.s), *Anatolian Interfaces: Hittites, Greeks and their Neighbours: Proceedings of an International Conference on Cross-Cultural Interaction, September 17-19, 2004*, Oxford, 117–122.
- 2010. "Writing" in Hieroglyphic Luwian. In: Singer, I. (ed*.) ipamati kistamati pari tumatimis, Luwian and Hittite Studies presented to J. David Hawkins on the occasion of his 70th birthday*, Emery and Claire Yass Publications in Archaeology, Institute of Archaeology, Tel Aviv University, Tel Aviv. 182–187.
- 2012. Iron Age Hieroglyphic Luwian Inscriptions. WAW 29, Atlanta.
- forthcoming. Schrift und Schriftlichkeit. Die anatolische Hieroglyphenschrift.

Penney, J.H.W.,
- 2004. Indo-European Perspectives. Studies in Honour of Anna Morpurgo Davies, Oxford.

Plöchl, R.,
- 2003. *Einführung ins Hieroglyphen-Luwische*, DBH Band 8.

Poetto, M.,
- 1979. Luvio geroglifico SAR+*r(à)* KAT-*ta*, *Fs Szemerényi*, 669–677.
- *Luvio mana- 'vedere': eteo meni/a- 'viso'*, in: Etter A. (ed.), *o-o-pe-ro-si. Festschrift für Ernst Risch zum 75. Geburtstag*, Berlin - New York,125-128

Rieken, E.,
- 1994. Der Wechsel *-a-/-i-* in der Stammbildung des hethitischen Nomens, *HS* 107, 42–53.
- 1999. *Untersuchungen zur nominalen Stammbildung des Hethitischen*, StBoT 44, Wiesbaden.
- 2004. Das Präteritum des Medio-Passivs im Hieroglyphen-Luwischen, *HS* 117/2, 179–188.

- 2005. Neues zum Ursprung der anatolischen i-Mutation, *HS* 118, 48–74.
- 2006. Zum hethitisch-luwischen Sprachkontakt in historischer Zeit, *AoF* 33, 271–85.
- 2007. Hieroglyphen-luwisch *i-zi-ia-*: ein Beitrag zur Rekonstruktion der urindogermanischen Kulturgeschichte, in: Hock, W. and Meier-Brügger, M. (eds.), Daru Slovesiny. Festschrift für Christoph Koch zum 65. Geburtstag, Munich, 263–275.
- 2008. Die Zeichen <ta>, <tá> und <tà> in den hieroglyphen-luwischen Inschriften der Nachgro"reichszeit, in: Archi, A. and Francia, R. (eds.), Atti del 6o Congresso di Ittitologia, SMEA 50/2, 637–47.

Rieken, E. and Yakubovich, I.,
- 2010. The New Values of Luwian Signs L 319 And L 175. In: Singer, I. (ed.) *ipamati kistamati pari tumatimis, Luwian and Hittite Studies presented to J. David Hawkins on the occasion of his 70th birthday*, Emery and Claire Yass Publications in Archaeology, Institute of Archaeology, Tel Aviv University, Tel Aviv, 199-219.

Sayce, A.H.,
- 1903. *The Hittites, The Story of a Forgotten Empire*, London.

Schmidt, G.,
- 1988. Griechisch ἔνθα, ἔνθεν in: *Gs Herter*, 224–226.

Simon, Z.
- 2008. Towards an interpretation of the hieroglyphic Luwian pair of signs *109.*285 and the phonetic value of *448, *Kadmos* 47, 20–30.
- 2009. Where is the Land of Sura of the Hieroglyphic Luwian Inscription KARKAMIŠ A4b and Why Were Cappadocians Called Syrians by Greeks, *AoF* 39, 167–180.
- in Vorbereitung[1]. Der phonetische Wert der luwischen Laryngale*, in: 8HitCongrTagungsakten des VIII. Hethitologiekongreß, 5.-9. September 2011, Warschau.
- in Vorbereitung[2]. Once again on the Hieroglyphic Luwian sign *19 <á>.

Singer, I.,
- 2010. (ed.) *ipamati kistamati pari tumatimis, Luwian and Hittite Studies presented to J. David Hawkins on the occasion of his 70th birthday*, Emery and Claire Yass Publications in Archaeology, Institute of Archaeology, Tel Aviv University, Tel Aviv.

Starke, F.,
- 1979. Zu den hethitischen und luwischen Verbalabstrakta auf -,*sfa-*, *KZ* 93, 247–261.
- 1982. Die Kasusendungen der luwischen Sprachen, *Fs Neumann*, 407–425.

- 1985. *Die keilschrift-luwischen Texte in Umschrift*, StBoT 30, Wiesbaden.
- 1990. *Untersuchung zur Stammbildung des keilschrift-luwischen Nomens*, StBoT 31, Wiesbaden.

Tekoğlu, R., and Lemaire, A.,
- 2000. La bilingue royale louvito-phénicienne de Çineköy, Académie des Inscriptions & Belles-Lettres, comptes rendus, 961–1007.

Weitenberg, J.J.S.,
- 1984. *Die hethitischen u-Stämme*, Amsterdam.

Yakubovich, I.
- 2008a. The Luvian Enemy, *Kadmos* 47, 1–19.
- 2008b. Hittite-Luvian Bilingualism and the Origin of Anatolian Hieroglyphs, in Kazansky, N.N. (ed.), Acta Linguistica Petropolitana, Transactions of the Institute for Linguistic Studies, Vol. IV, part 1, St. Petersburg, 9–36.
- 2008c. The origin of Luwian possessive Adjectives, Proceedings of the 19th Annual UCLA Indo-European Conference, Jones-Bley, K. (et al. ed.), Journal of Indo-European Studies Monograph Series No. 54, 193–217.
- 2010a. Sociolinguistics of the Luvian Language, University of Chicago PhD dissertation, http://oi.uchicago.edu/research/library/dissertation
- 2010b, The West Semitic God El in Anatolian Hieroglyphic Transmission, in: Cohen, Y., Gilan, A., Miller J.L. (eds.), *Pax Hethitica. Studies on the Hittites and Their Neighbours in Honour of Itamar Singer*, Wiesbaden, 385–98.

10   Luwian Poetry

To state emphatically, here we enter the realms of fiction. The following text is
a modern fake of well-known provenance, a contribution for Eisenbraun's 2008
Ancient Near Eastern Valentine Contest. The drawing on the cover is an attempt
to render the poem in hieroglyphs but feel free to carve your own stele...

§ 1   MAGNUS.DOMINA *na-wa/i+ra/i-li* TERRA-REL+*ra/i-i*
        "ANIMAL.EQUUS"-*s™u-sà-ta-la-u-na* (LITUUS)á-*za-ti*
§ 2   ("ANIMAL.BESTIA")*HWI-sa₅+ra/i-pa HWI-sa* ("PANIS")*ma-li-ri+i-*
        mi-i-sá ("*478")*ku-tú-pi-li-sa*
§ 3   *sa+ra/i-ku-sa* ANIMAL.LEO REL+*ra/i* (ANIMAL)GAZELLA-*na*
        INFRA-*ta* (EDERE)*pa-sa-i*
§ 4   HASTARIUS *sa-i a-ta-ni-ha* *274-*i*
§ 5   *wa/i+ra/i-pa-li-sa* HEROS URBS-*si* PORTA VERSUS-*na* (PES₂)*a-wi-ti*
§ 6   ARHA-*ha u-sa-nu-wa/i-mi-za* DEUS.DOMUS-*za a-ta* LITUUS-*na-ti-i*
§ 7   FLAMMAE(?) *ki-nu-wa/i-ti-i* (PANIS.PITHOS)*a-za-li-ya* (PES₂)*a-wi*
§ 8   STELE (CRUS)*ta-za-tu mu-wa/i-ta-li-za-ha* CASTRUM-*za mu-wa/i*
§ 9   *a-ma-za* EXERCITUS-*za sa₅-ni* ENSIS PRAE-*i pi-ia-wa/i*
§ 10   EGO REL-*ti* MILLE-*su ARHA* MORI (*462)*mu-wa/i-i-tà-sa-ha*
        CORNU+*RA/I-i* (PES₂)*a-wi-ti*

§ 1   My Lady loves to ride in foreign territory
§ 2   But fear the wild animals, o honey-sweet lamb!
§ 3   As the mighty lion swallows up the gazelle,
§ 4   The lance-carrier shoots and smites the enemy.
§ 5   The brave hero comes to the city gates
§ 6   And beholds the mighty-blessed temple.
§ 7   The flame burns, come to the feast!
§ 8   Let the stele continue to stand and conquer the mighty fortress,
§ 9   Overthrow my army and I will hand over the sword
§ 10   So that I shall die a thousand times and the seed will come to fullness.